THE TREES ARE
ALL YOUNG ON
GARRISON HILL

Detail from a portrait of the author by Michael Noakes 1989

THE TREES ARE
ALL YOUNG ON
GARRISON HILL

An exploration of war and memory

Gordon Graham

THE KOHIMA EDUCATIONAL TRUST

© The Kohima Educational Trust
5 Beechwood Drive
Marlow
Buckinghamshire SL7 2DH
UK

ISBN 0-9552687-0-2

First published in 2005 in an edition limited to **726**
one thousand copies, of which this is number ....

Index compiled by Hazel Bell
Maps by John Mitchell
Designed by Douglas Williamson
Printed by Martins the Printers, Berwick upon Tweed
Bound by Hunter and Foulis, Edinburgh
Distributed by Horizons Bookshop, Marlow

Foreword

ALL TOO OFTEN, accounts of battles in which one was involved leave one protesting, 'But it wasn't *like* that!' The chapters of Gordon Graham's memoir which deal with the part played by the 1st Battalion Queen's Own Cameron Highlanders in the Battle of Kohima and the subsequent advance into Burma not only tells how it was, but also conveys the authentic atmosphere. Reading it sixty years later, I vividly recall those stirring days when the formidable Japanese 31st Division erupted into Assam and laid siege to the little town in the Naga Hills where was fought what one Japanese combatant called 'that great, bitter battle'.

The 1st Cameron Highlanders had spent the previous two years in India, training for combined operations. As Gordon describes, officers on Indian rates of pay were well off and enjoyed a certain amount of social acceptance from the British community. The soldiers, on the other hand, were paid a pittance, and as in Kipling's day, were ignored. The result was that the soldiers – mainly conscripts of some education – loathed the country and the expatriate British, and despised the natives. That the 2nd Division, of which the Camerons were part, was to fight so well at Kohima, under-gunned and unsupported as it was for the first few weeks, stems from what Gordon believes was 'the innate decency, discipline, pride of regiment, and comradeship' of the soldiers. He is right.

To me at any rate, Gordon epitomised the 'Happy Warrior'. He writes of the 'relish for war' that he discerned when taking over a position from the Sikhs of the 1st Patiala Infantry on the Shenam defences after we reached Imphal. Looking back, I would now say the same of Gordon. He certainly gave me the impression that he was enjoying the war. It was only on reading his manuscript that I realised that he himself had suffered the earlier loss of his brother, and at the height of the Kohima battle, of his father. Of this, he gave no outward sign whatsoever. And only on reading his story did I appreciate the deep affection and warm regard he had for the men under his command – and indeed, for all of us.

Endowed with personal courage above the average, he had the gift of making those around him feel brave too. He was also highly competent; things always went better when Gordon was around. Gordon Graham was, in fact, a born soldier, although to be candid, I do not think he could have put up with life in the regular army for long. The Cameron Highlanders treasured too many, to use his words, 'arcane rituals'.

His daughter Sylvia's account of the pilgrimage that she undertook with her husband Robert to follow in the footsteps of her father and the Cameron Highlanders from Kohima in Assam to Mount Popa in central Burma sets this memoir apart. They undertook the journey in their own time and at their own expense, 'heart drawn to see where great things were suffered and done for them'.* They clearly have the same zest for a challenge as Gordon. The reception they received from the Naga community confirmed its welcome for the Kohima Educational Trust, to which Gordon has generously assigned the copyright and all profits from this book. Thus those of us who fought at Kohima can partly discharge some of the debt we owe to this outstanding race.

The Naga friend to whom Gordon first wrote about the idea of the Trust said in his response, 'You have not forgotten us,' illustrating how war and memory – a theme Gordon explores in his story – can give a positive meaning to a violent past.

Lt Col David Murray
Oxton, Berwickshire, July 2005

*In great deeds something abides. On great fields something stays. Forms change and pass: bodies disappear: but spirits linger, to consecrate ground for the vision place of souls. And reverent men and women from afar, and generations that know us not and that we know not of, heart drawn to see where and by whom great things were suffered and done for them, shall come to this deathless field to ponder and dream; and lo! the shadow of a mighty presence shall wrap them in its bosom, and the power of the vision shall pass into their souls.

Gettysburg Oration 1889
General JOSHUA LAWRENCE CHAMBERLAIN, United States Army

Contents

LIST OF ILLUSTRATIONS

MAPS

Preface

I FIRST WROTE THIS BOOK as a war memoir of the years 1939 to 1946. It began as notes for my daughter Sylvia and son-in-law Robert when they set out at the end of 2001 on an adventurous trip to trace the battle route of the 1st Cameron Highlanders in the Burma Campaign of 1944–45. Excerpts from the diary Sylvia kept of their travels in Nagaland, Manipur and Burma are interpolated into the narrative under the title *Footsteps*.

Discussing the manuscript with friends and family, I realized it was lacking in context. Who was this person to whom these things happened, and why did he react as he did? Going to war is a time-shift, a disruption not of the individual's choosing, which persists in memory as a sort of lifelong spiritual jetlag. Even if you take up where you left off, even if you do what you had planned to do before interruption, but even more if the experience leads you, as in my case, into a life pattern undreamt of, the returned soldier is not the same person who went to war.

In the accumulation of memories as we get old, those of war are out of kilter with the rest. There is an urge to record them, as a kind of extraterrestrial episode, like one's personal moon-landing. We reveal this in our attitude towards wars as dividing lines in life spans. My parents' generation, born towards the end of the 19th century, commonly spoke of life 'before the war' and 'after the war'. My own generation, born in the aftermath of World War I, were children of the 20th century who grew up believing that the century's crisis had happened before we were born. Some war veterans pretend that this time divisor never happened: 'He never talks about it.' But memory of war does not go away, no matter how busy one's subsequent life. If anything, it becomes more vivid.

Behind the thousands of old comrades' reminiscences, military histories, autobiographies, as well as the reunions, memorial services, marches and salutes adjuring the survivors and their descendants to remember the war-dead, lie memory-inspired quests for explanation and reassurance. Immediately after a war there is celebration of victory and joy over the return of peace. Early post-war literature tends to romanticize the war experience. Later, the memories of those who participated and the attention paid by the following generations centre round sacrifice and suffering. What led to the sacrifice and suffering – of both sides in any war – and how a better understanding of these causes can have contemporary relevance, are too seldom addressed.

Memory is not just a comforter; it also asks the question: how can the past come to the aid of the present and lend more hope to the future? This search for continuity led me to frame my memoir between a youthful autobiography, *Before the Beginning*, and a concluding chapter, *After the End*, which relates how the memories of war surfaced in unplanned ways and at serendipitous moments during the rest of my life.

DEDICATED TO THE MEN OF THE 1ST BATTALION
THE QUEEN'S OWN CAMERON HIGHLANDERS
WHO DIED DURING THE BURMA CAMPAIGN
OF 1944 AND 1945

LOCHABER NO MORE

Tom and Marion Graham with their sons, Gordon (*left*) and Tommy, on holiday at Shiskine, Isle of Arran, 1934

Chapter One

Before the Beginning

The childhood shows the man
As morning shows the day
JOHN MILTON *Paradise Regained*

GLASGOW BETWEEN THE WORLD WARS was a city notorious for crime and grime, but at its heart was an aspiring Victorian middle class, into which my mother, Marion Hutcheson, had been born in 1882. She was the eldest and most ambitious of a family of seven (three sisters and four brothers), a quarrelsome brood, whom Marion aggravated by being censorious and superior. Their father, a coal and timber merchant, was briefly prosperous when he pioneered the delivery of coal to peoples' houses in horse-drawn carts from which it was hefted in hundredweight bags on the leather-padded shoulders of the cart drivers. But he drank too much, spent money carelessly and died young.

Marion graduated from school at sixteen and stayed on as a teacher's assistant while training to be a dressmaker. In 1906 she went to London where, in applying for a job at Debenham & Freebody's department store, she was greatly incensed to be told by the manager, 'We don't employ people from the provinces.' Marion, a tall, flaming redhead, drew herself to her full height. 'Glasgow is not the provinces. It is the second city of the Empire.' She got the job at 22s 6d a week – enough to maintain herself at the YWCA, where she roomed with a milliner from Southampton, named Edith Fry, who became a lifelong friend.

Living in London for two years gave Marion freedom from family quarrels and the intellectual scope she craved. Among her leisure activities, she joined a reading circle; went to a different church every Sunday; heard George Bernard Shaw lecture; was in the crowd applauding Winston Churchill as he emerged from the church with his bride Clementine, and read the entire works of Robert Browning. In my boyhood, astonishingly, she introduced me to the 19th Century New England writers – Longfellow, Louisa

May Alcott, Whitman, Thoreau, Hawthorne. This was after I had read, with her encouragement, the works of Scott, Dickens and Thackeray as well as minor Victorian writers like George Gissing and Mrs Gaskell.

My father Tom was the opposite of Marion – quiet, modest and respectful of knowledge without any aspirations to learning. Born in 1883 in Hawick, a hill-enfolded textile town in the Scottish Borders, he had left school at fourteen to be apprenticed to a draper. He was the eldest of nine, four sisters and five brothers, who lived in harmony with one another all their lives. Their father had been an engine driver who became a guard. In his driving days he would sound the train's whistle when it passed the family home beginning its slow haul through the Cheviot Hills. Long after he had gone, I lay awake in the upstairs room listening for the hoot of a steam engine in the darkness, a sound of loneliness reassured.

In his young days, my grandfather's duties had taken him to Fife and onward to Dundee. Providentially, he was off duty on the night of the Tay Bridge disaster in 1879, by which year he was courting my paternal grandmother, Mary Ritchie, daughter of a farmer's grieve. Born in 1850, she was by then in service in a big house near Anstruther. Grandma Graham was the only grandparent I knew. A dignified matriarch, dressed always in full-length black skirt, white ruffled blouse, her grey hair gathered in a meticulous bun, she lived till she died in 1936 in the grey granite terraced house on the hill near the railway, cared for by her spinster daughters who were also to see out their days in the family home.

Tom left Hawick in 1904 to take a job in Glasgow in the textiles department of Campbell, Stewart and McDonald, a wholesale warehouse. In a letter dated February 8, 1904 from Myrtle Cottage, Pittenweem, Tom's maternal grandmother wished him well in the big city. Clear in handwriting, correct in spelling and grammar, simple in vocabulary, she hopes 'you will keep well and trust you will get on all right, but I think there is no fear of you. It is a good thing you have got lodging that you think looks so comfortable and so near your work. I hope the young man you are to share your room with is as nice a fellow as the landlady says and trust you will feel comfortable.' She complains that the spout over her back door is overflowing and 'the landlady does not want to put up a new one'. This letter, given to me by my Aunt Mary, my father's youngest sister, eighty-five years after it was written, is the entire Graham archive. All else was discreetly destroyed. Family business was private.

Tom and Marion met at a Presbyterian church social some time after Marion returned from London. In Tom, with whom she was to spend the middle third of her ninety-seven years, Marion found the stability and respectability her family lacked. He was handsome withal, his Greek-like features enhanced by a butter-pointed moustache, although he was already balding at twenty-seven years old. In Marion ('My dearest Myn') Tom found someone sophisticated, artistic, musical, well-read, smartly dressed (she made her own clothes all her life) and who was never backward in being forward. She was the decision-maker. Tom was her quiet partner. He liked to get up in the morning, clean the shoes (my brother's and mine as well as his own) and make the porridge for breakfast while whistling to himself.

In 1912 Tom was sent to South Africa to represent his firm. Marion followed two years later. They were married in the white Presbyterian Church overlooking Camps Bay, a suburb of Cape Town, on June 2, 1914. They settled in Klerksdorp, a mining town in the Transvaal, from which Tom travelled all over the country, sometimes by bullock cart, with his samples of fabrics in black fibre boxes. I still have one in the attic.

My brother Tommy was born in 1915. In the same year, Tom lost his job, trade between Britain and South Africa having shrunk because of the war, and was hired as store manager by one of his customers. Without being rich, the Grahams led the privileged life of colonials in South Africa. Marion loved it, although she had reservations about 'the Boers'. At the end of 1919 they made what Marion described for the rest of her life as their greatest mistake: they returned to Scotland. South Africa became her paradise lost. My brother and I would squirm inwardly when Marion prefaced some criticism of life in Scotland with, 'When we were in South Africa ...'. Tom had been offered a partnership in the store where he was working, but he was not a risk-taker. Later, diamonds were discovered there. He could have been rich, but instead returned to his old job at Campbell, Stewart and McDonald, where in due course, he became a departmental manager and served for the rest of his life. He remained a wage earner; never had a bank account; brought his weekly earnings home in an envelope each Friday night and handed it to Marion. 'There you are, my dear.' His annual income in 1939 was £475.

My arrival in 1920 increased the congestion in the tenement flat off Victoria Road, a street of bustling shops and clanking tramcars on the south side of Glasgow, where we were lodging with Marion's mother and one of her sisters, a cohabitation from which Tom and Marion were desperate to extricate themselves and their sons. Tom's job required frequent travel to places like Kidderminster to buy carpets, or High Wycombe to buy furniture, or London to buy home furnishings. He was away in 1922 when Marion found a flat with an affordable rent. However, she said in a telegram to Tom, the owners wanted £400 for 'a few sticks of furniture'. 'Take it', he telegraphed back.

Our new home, three floors up, had three bedrooms and a triangular kitchen heated by a coal-fire range. In the kitchen's apex corner was a box-bed, a cosy retreat from which to observe and be observed. My earliest memory of 77 Albert Avenue was being circumcised on the kitchen counter. I cried.

Accessed, like all Glasgow tenements, through a 'close' – a grim ground-floor passageway – No 77 had two flats on each of its four floors, joined by stone stairways scrubbed weekly by the house-proud tenants. In the back yard there was a wash-house with a steam boiler and iron posts for clothes lines, all of which the eight housewives put to vigorous use on their allotted half-days.

The tenement was opposite the local church, a grey, confident, steepled landmark. Behind the church was a piece of wasteland which we called 'the backies', where the local children drew lines with chalk on the walls to represent stumps for cricket which we played with an old bat and a rubber ball. Queen's Park, with its playgrounds, swings, shrubs and paths, and open-air arena where concert parties performed on summer afternoons, was only a block away. Adjacent to the park was a public pond where I sailed my model yacht. Neighbourhood children played in the middle of the street. There were few cars.

When I was five I was enrolled at a primary school in Battlefield, a neighbouring suburb on the other side of the park, so called after the battle of Langside, where the supporters of Mary Queen of Scots made their last stand before she fled to imprisonment and execution. She was one of the mythical figures in my childhood pantheon, almost all of whom happened to be Scottish – national sentiment excusing bland distortions of history. Others included William Wallace, Robert the Bruce, Rob Roy and Bonnie Prince Charlie, all of whom were alleged to have fought, usually as losers, against English 'oppressors'. Victorious battles such as Bannock-burn or Prestonpans were glorified. Defeats such as Flodden or Culloden were the result of English perfidy or overwhelming force.

For the Scottish pre-adolescent of the late 1920s, these historical heroes met competition from the movies ('the pictures' as we called them). Films about Tom Mix and his horse Silver King, with piano accompaniment, at Saturday morning matinees gave credence to our childhood games, cowboys as the 'goodies' and Indians as the 'baddies'.

When I was eight, I followed my brother to Hutchesons' Boys' Grammar School, a day school half a mile south of the River Clyde. Established by two brothers Hutcheson in green fields in 1641, by the 1920s it was surrounded by the Gorbals, Glasgow's most notorious slum. Defended by a spiked iron fence, and with its pillared portico leading to an entrance hall and mahogany-bannistered stairway, the dark grey school building looked more like a run-down courthouse than a school. Scholastically, however, it was in the upper bracket. Four subjects – Latin, Greek, English and mathematics – formed the core of the curriculum. Other subjects were ancillary. The teachers, impudently given nicknames such as 'Tubby' Smith, 'Puggy' Maclennan, 'Soapy' Somerville, 'Pony' Milne and 'Stink Pot' Ferguson, were dedicated scholars and decisive disciplinarians. For misdemeanours, the strap, with four tails and made from layers of black leather sewn together to give it the stiffness of a board, was administered summarily on the palm of the hand – a minimum of two strokes and a maximum of six. It was feared, but not resented.

Sports were a low priority, which was sad for my brother Tommy, who excelled at any game involving a ball.

In 1927 we had moved to a substantial red sandstone terrace house in Netherlee, on the southern outskirts of the city, a move made possible less by increased affluence than by disciplined living. Marion would always buy yesterday's loaf at the baker – it was 'easier to cut'. It was also a penny cheaper. We ate well (four meals a day) and plates were always emptied. Garbage cans were small.

For Marion the move to Netherlee signalled the final (she hoped) emancipation from the toils of her dysfunctional family. Four of her siblings had by that time emigrated to Australia, more as refugees from the depression than as pioneers. When she met the other two, conversation tended to become acrimonious and degenerate into tight-lipped insults. A sister who returned from Australia with a child but no husband was arrested for shoplifting. Their mother hanged herself. From all such family shame my brother and I were carefully shielded. I did not learn of my grandmother's suicide until after Marion died in 1979. For Tommy and me, family meant the Grahams, the brothers with their wives and children, who gathered every Christmas at the family home in Hawick. On one such occasion, at the age of four, I made my first after-dinner speech. With my head at table-height, I had found that my observations were unheard amid the buzz of adult merriment. So I stood on my chair and raised my voice to pronounce the childhood equivalent of 'If I may say a few words'. My actual words were 'Me wanna peak'. The sudden silence was most gratifying and taught me the first lesson in public speaking: make sure your audience is listening before you say anything. Unfortunately, I had not learned the second lesson, which is to have something to say, and sat down in confusion.

In my teen years I cycled each summer the ninety miles from Glasgow to Hawick, to stay for weeks in the dormer-windowed upstairs bedroom, with its ewer and basin for ablutions and its view over the apple tree and roses in the garden, across the 'auld grey toon' to the hills. On the skyline stood an isolated hawthorn tree shaped by the wind. Every time I returned to Hawick in later life, I drove to Linden Crescent to check that the tree had withstood the elements and the encroaching township. The population of Hawick has not grown. The railway line has been grassed or built over. Synthetics have eroded the market for woollen garments and the Chinese have learned to weave their own cashmere. When I bought a sweater in Beijing in 1987, I thought of the unemployment in Hawick, and felt such a twinge of conscience that I bought two sweaters in the mill shops there the next time I passed through.

The only slight shadow between Tom and Marion and his family arose from Marion's conversion to Christian Science, with which Tom meekly went along, although it meant his giving up smoking. His sisters signified genteel disapproval by refraining from any reference to the subject. Marion had initially been attracted by the aura of calm certainty surrounding the ladies who formed the majority of the Church's adherents, and subsequently by the promise of spiritual healing. The teachings of Mary Baker Eddy, who founded the Christian Science movement in New England in the late 19th century, gained thousands of adherents in Scotland in the 1920s and 30s. Grafted onto the plain living and high thinking of Presbyterianism, Christian Science pervaded my upbringing with love and discipline in equal measure. No medication was allowed. In times of illness, a practitioner was called to do 'mental work' on the patient's behalf by drawing attention to the erroneous beliefs that cause disease and invoking the power of the Divine Mind. Marion's practitioner was a strong-minded lady from Milwaukee, given to imperious declarations of truth which did not invite argument. Among the statements in Mrs Eddy's textbook is one to the effect that mankind will come to salvation 'either through Science or suffering'. On one occasion, when I had had a tooth extracted without anaesthetic, I remarked to my mother that she seemed to do the Science while I did the suffering.

Nurtured thus in a boyhood both sheltered and spartan, my adolescence was shaped alike by a catalogue of prohibitions and by lack of opportunity to transgress. Telling lies, swearing and gambling were among the easier no-no's. The top of Marion's sin list was liquor. Tom's suppliers gave him the option of a ham or half a dozen bottles of whisky at Christmas time. We had a lot of hams. Once whisky arrived by mistake and Marion poured it down the sink. Among the seven deadlies, I had little trouble with sloth or envy, there was no scope for gluttony and I was too priggish to re-cognize pride. Lust was not listed, fornication being too far off the screen to be mentioned in our household, and my post-puberty urges caused me secret shame which going to a boys' school did nothing to alleviate. My first conversations with girls as fellow human beings occurred at the university. Until then my bicycle, on which I rode alone with tent and primus stove over much of Scotland, was my childhood sweetheart. When the frame broke on my first bike, I was bereft. Tom brought home a catalogue and let me choose the model I wanted, which was the most expensive (£5) – a Raleigh touring model with a Sturmey Archer three-speed gear. It was to carry me thousands of miles. And sometimes I carried *it*, since I enjoyed crossing roadless mountain passes. You could live on a shilling a day in the 1930s if you slept out and liked porridge.

The bicycle had been a vehicle of liberation for Marion who at the end of the 19th century had enthusiastically joined what the male chauvinists of the day dismissed as young women's 'cycling craze', which in the event was a precursor of the suffragette move-ment. Cycle touring in the 1930s was similarly a liberator for schoolboys of the time longing for adventure and independence.

Tommy and I had an upbringing in which much stress was laid on outward signs of inward virtue – to be tidy, to have clean nails and good manners, and, most importantly, to speak grammatically. Marion was determined that her sons should not have a Glasgow accent. Dropped consonants and broadened vowels were pounced upon. The *Grammar* in our school's title was not theoretical: verbs, weak and strong, were conjugated; nouns, proper and common, were declined; adjectives, regular and irregular, compared. Marion had a repertoire of precepts which contrived to combine moral duty with economic prudence, such as: 'Do the thing you have to do before the thing you want to do' or 'If you use what you have, you'll never want.' There was no consumer society. We were pious and orderly. Returning from our annual summer holiday at the seaside, Marion would say, 'It's nice to get back to a regular way of doing things.'

I reached adolescence with little perception that I had been born in the aftermath of a world war, and with no perception at all that the clouds of another one were gathering. Censorship during World War I had glossed over the horrors of trench warfare. Memories of combat were bottled up. Armistice Day – as Remembrance Sunday was then called – the poppies, the two minutes' silence, parades and services ending with *The Last Post*, jogged public memory once a year, not about the causes and consequences of war but about our duty to honour the glorious dead. War, insofar as it was discussed, was represented to our young ears as more heroic than tragic. Books such as T E Lawrence's *Seven Pillars of Wisdom*, or Ian Hay's *First Hundred Thousand* or John Buchan's *Mr Standfast* represented war as more adventure than folly. Rupert Brooke's poem *The Soldier* resonated more than Vera Brittain's *Testament of Youth*. The Treaty of Versailles was no more than the Germans deserved. In any case, it all belonged to The Past.

I was awakened from these delusions when I went to the university in 1937. Being neither bowler-hat nor cloth-cap, I joined the university's Liberal Party and was rapidly educated into the implications of the Nazi occupation of the Rhineland, the Spanish Civil War and Mussolini's invasion of Abyssinia. The Austrian *Anschluss* and the Munich crisis deepened our forebodings, on all of which, being students, we were vociferous. In my second and third years as an undergraduate, I became successively secretary and president of the university's Liberal Club, which engineered the election of Sir Archibald Sinclair, leader of the parliamentary Liberal Party, as Lord Rector of the University – an honorary but politically symbolic post.

Politics at the university was, of course, extra-curricular, as were rugby, badminton, fencing, rock climbing, the choral society and playing straight-man to the comedian in the touring *College Pudding* revue. But I was fortunate also to have an emancipatory curriculum: Greek, Latin, Logic, Political Economy and Moral Philosophy. Suddenly I was my own intellectual master and could question everything, which I did volubly. The shackles of school and church dropped away. I became friends with Roman Catholics, atheists, Jews, communists, Africans, European refugees. It was intoxicating. My parents, bless them, released me from my childhood regimen.

Marion was happy that her scholastic hopes for her younger son had been fulfilled, and became reconciled to the path of her first-born who was by then a champion golfer, an international triallist at rugby, a handsome devil dashing around the town in plus fours on his motor cycle and keeping company with a glamorous girl from the upper reaches of society.

As for Tom, he thought both his sons were wonderful, whatever we did. We had proud parents who lived for their sons as much as for each other. Our chosen worlds (I planned to take a law degree and become an advocate) lay before us.

Chapter Two

Enlistment

Something tells me I am needed
At the front to fight the foe
Boer War Music Hall song

FEW SETTINGS for the end of innocence could rival the mountains of north-west Scotland in brilliant summer weather. I spent most of August 1939 as guide to an international group of students, walking and climbing. We stayed in youth hostels and did our own cooking. The group included Pierre, a blond, blue-eyed Frenchman who was mad about rock-climbing; a Viennese Jewish refugee couple; a beautiful Scottish girl called Morris Cameron, with whom I sang duets as we walked and who became my first love; and a 28-year-old German called Peter Konig, a school teacher, for whom I formed great respect and with whom I exchanged addresses.

A week after we parted, Peter and I were officially enemies. In spite of my supposed political sophistication, the declaration of war took me by surprise. There had been so many false alarms, and we all had the optimism of the insulated. I had met and revered mature students who had fought with the International Brigade in the Spanish Civil War. I had presided at a concert given by Czech student refugees from the Nazi occupation of their homeland. In debates I had made fiery speeches against appeasement. But Europe still seemed distant. At the age of nineteen I had been out of Scotland only twice, once to welcome my parents on their return from their silver wedding trip to South Africa, and once to visit my brother who had a job in Lancaster. I was a Scots provincial, and a tad self-righteous to boot. For nine years, in the words of the Hutchesons' school song, I had 'bent my will to the grim book drill for the good of body and soul', and was now embarking on my third year at the university. While I might have views on world events, I did not expect them to interfere with my life. War had finished in 1918, and subsequent distant wars were matters for indignation, not apprehension.

So when on the evening of September 3 I looked through a window of our darkened house to the darkened streets, with the occasional headlight-shaded car creeping by, it was a shock. Next morning I told my parents I was going to enlist. At the University, a hurriedly-formed committee of professors was interviewing volunteers to select those considered to be 'potential officers'. This meant that you joined up as a private soldier in a squad given an especially hard time to weed out non-qualifiers. I was interviewed on September 5. When they asked me which of the services I wished to join, it did not occur to me to say anything other than the infantry. I went straight from the interview for a medical examination and waited for my call-up papers ... and waited. After some weeks, a letter came from the War Office. They were not accepting volunteers who were shortly due to graduate. Some war! I was deflated. My parents were relieved. Along with the rest of the British nation we slid into that quasi-normality which became known as the *Phoney War*.

In the winter of 1939 and through the spring of 1940, most of Britain laboured under the threat, but did not suffer the impact, of war. We had conscription, the blackout, rationing, air-raid sirens, barrage balloons, but no bombs. Children were evacuated to the country. Strange-looking soldiers appeared on the streets of Glasgow – French *chasseurs* wearing berets and baggy trousers and Poles in smart uniforms. Commando troops in training took over sections of the Scottish Highlands.

I continued my collegiate life, attempting to direct my studies and recreation towards preparation for military service. My two new subjects, Roman Law and International Law, could not have been less relevant. I became a part-time apprentice-at-law to a firm of solicitors, my principal duty being to collect rents in the slums, which caused me to wonder, in my innocence, how the weekly ready envelope of the douce could be next door to the chronic arrears of the poor, whom I snobbishly regarded as feckless. In my free time I went mountaineering, rock-climbing, camping at snowy altitudes, alone or with my friend Jimmy Mitchell, a divinity student. He and I and four others founded the Glasgow University Mountaineering Club in 1938. In Burma in 1944 I met Pat

Four of the six founders of the Glasgow University Mountaineering Club, (*left to right*) Alex Honeyman, the author, Jimmy Mitchell and Boyd Anderson, 1938

Hamilton, another member of our group, who told me that Jimmy, who as a pacifist had been conscripted into forestry work, had fallen off the Shelter Stone Crag in the Cairngorms and been killed. Smiling, gentle Jimmy has always been somehow on my conscience, because I introduced him to rock climbing.

During that winter, as President of the University's Liberal Club, I alarmed my parents by making speeches critical of the conduct of the war. Shocked heads turned when I asked from the back of the hall at a by-election meeting why British soldiers' lives were being thrown away in Norway.

My time at the university had made me a political animal, and had also put my religious upbringing in philosophical context. Reading Leibniz, Schopenhauer, Kant and Bishop Berkeley emancipated me from dogma. I met intellectual Catholics with whom I debated the immaculate conception, and learned tolerance of and respect for the views of others. Joining a group of students sitting round the fireplace in the Union, the students' club at the foot of Gilmorehill, I would find one enumerating points on his fingers as he developed his argument that there was no God, while his theist opponent listened and awaited his turn to challenge and refute.

Another powerful influence was my study of Classical Greek and its literature, for which I had wonderful teachers at school and university. This study was not all book learning. At school we put on plays by Aeschylus and Aristophanes. I once played Iphigenia and remember the cardboard armour of Orestes scratching my chin as I murmured sweet nothings in his ear. Plato, Socrates and Aristotle provided me with the rationale for dialogue. The Aristotelian mean, 'Know thyself, nothing in excess' made a great impression on me, as did the works of Thucydides, the first soldier-historian.

The unexpected third year at the university was a bonus of self-discovery. I paid scant attention to my studies, just managing to graduate. I would normally have gone on to take a Bachelor of Laws degree, but the dull paperwork of my apprenticeship turned me off the idea of a career in law. I wrote poetry and suffered pangs of virginal love, while waiting for war to start.

My impatience and frustration reached a peak in June after Dunkirk. I wrote an indignant letter to the War Office demanding to be called up. Whether as a result of this or merely as part of the general post-Dunkirk panic, an order finally arrived requiring me to report to Strensall Camp near York on July 18, 1940, the day after my twentieth birthday.

On the train to York, I met Neil White, a fellow Glaswegian, educated at the Leys School in Cambridge and a student at the university there. We were the same age. We were to spend the next five years in close comradeship. We were privates together, cadets together, officers together. We fought in the same battles, won the same medals. I was to be his best man at his wedding in Adderbury in Oxfordshire in 1942 and he at mine in Bombay in 1943.

Neil was easygoing, earthy, competitive, convivial. I was prudish, serious, disciplined, a teetotaller. Neil excelled at sports and would have been an international rugby and hockey player if the war had not intervened. After the war, he finished his degree at Cambridge and went back to the Leys, where in the following forty years he became a latter-day Mr Chips. The last time I saw him, in the cottage where his second wife Celia nursed him lovingly in his terminal illness, he sat cheerfully through dinner hugging the bag which substituted for his digestive apparatus. He died in 1990 at the age of sixty-nine.

Unlike Neil, I had joined the army completely ignorant of its ways. The recruit camp at Strensall was stimulating and puzzling – stimulating because of the comradeship and sense of purpose, and puzzling because what we were taught seemed to have little relationship to the new strategy of Blitzkrieg. Infantry training drills had changed little since 1918. You polished your boots, drilled with your rifle and learned to move at the double. But at least we were doing something to prepare for this vaguely frightening, but still distant, war, which, whatever its terrors, had a rationale: our homeland was threatened.

On one training exercise I was handed a piece of wood cut in the shape of a bottle and sent up a tree. The rest of the squad was instructed to run under the tree holding a wooden partition above their heads. I was to practise dropping the wooden bottle precisely on a circle drawn in the middle of the partition. Thus we were taught how tanks could be destroyed by Molotov cocktails dropped into their turrets. How we enticed the enemy's tanks to drive with open turrets under the trees where we secreted ourselves was not explained.

We were always hungry. Neil and I used to try to be at the head of the queue for meals, gobble our food and dodge out of the back door to rejoin the queue, but we were generally spotted by the muscular, no-nonsense canteen ladies. Identified by the white tabs on our shoulders, potential officers were disliked by both the regulars and the wartime conscripts who would mutter insults as we marched past.

As potential officers we were given lectures about the theory of war. In the first of these, our Sandhurst-trained company commander emphasized the importance of 'fah-pah'. Coming from

Scotland, where due attention is given to the letter 'r', I took some time to translate this to 'fire-power'.

The language of the troops, on the other hand, was a shock to my puritanical upbringing. Next to me on the barrack-room floor on which we slept was the room orderly, an old lag called Fuck-Fuck Webster, his nickname signifying both his limited vocabulary and his fondness for recounting his sexual experiences. When our convoy called at Cape Town in 1942, whom should I find officiating on the dockside and wearing a corporal's stripes? 'Fuck-Fuck!' I said, 'how nice to see you again. Where did you get these stripes?' 'Ah woon 'em,' he replied. Many still-serving old regulars would have retired but for the war. Their leathery complexions prematurely wizened, their wariness of authority engrained by years of dull peacetime soldiering, they were experts at finding jobs which combined maximum comfort with minimum effort. This was not true of the regular Non-Commissioned Officers (NCOs) and Warrant Officers (WOs), who drilled us and taught us that soldiering is a profession. All the regulars were heavily into sex and booze, appetites to which I had not yet been introduced.

After two weeks in Strensall, I fell ill and lay perspiring in the sick bay for three days, refusing medication in accordance with my Christian Science upbringing.

Refusal of treatment was a new experience for the medical officer. He called in the Adjutant, Captain John Benn, son of Sir Ernest Benn, one of the political heroes of the Liberal Party. 'Got one of your lot here, John,' the MO said. We chatted and Captain Benn advised that I should be left alone. After I recovered, the Company Commander offered me sick leave, which I declined on the grounds that I hadn't really been sick.

On September 16, 1940, our company was rushed before dawn to an airfield ten miles away and scattered on the grass in prone positions surrounding the runway with our rifles at the ready. It was believed to be the day that Germany would invade Britain. Just as well that no airborne troops arrived, since none of us had yet learned to fire with live ammunition.

The Lee-Enfield .303-inch rifle was the totem around which all infantry training revolved. We had to learn how to carry it and how to drill with it, but first how to clean it. Each recruit was issued with a cord with a loop at the end, some oil and a small piece of flannel to pull through the barrel of his rifle. The sheen of these barrels would be carefully inspected at each day's parade. A speck on your barrel could earn you a day's 'jankers' (menial duties in off-hours). An important part of the drill was to learn how to take the bayonet at the correct angle from its scabbard on your belt and fix it to the end of the rifle. You were then invited to charge straw-filled dummies, into which you plunged and out of which then extracted your bayonet with a bloodthirsty yell. The last thing you were taught about the rifle was how to fire it. This involved parading at the firing range, where you were instructed to lie on your belly, legs apart, feet splayed. You were then shown how to sight the rifle on a target which obligingly remained stationary. Finally you were given a clip of five rounds of ammunition. Firing a rifle for the first time was a big shock. It hurts your shoulder. The secret is to squeeze the trigger gently and be ready for the recoil. The accuracy of your fire was measured by markers concealed in trenches below the targets, who waved flags signalling bull's eyes, inners, outers or washouts.

Later when we became officers, we were issued with .38-inch revolvers, which proved to be hazardous in Burma because they enabled the officers to be identified by the enemy. Also, you have to sight a revolver like a rifle, by which time, at close quarters in the jungle, you are dead. I also had my own weapon, a Smith & Wesson .45-inch revolver, given to me by the headmaster of my school when I went to his home to say goodbye. He had found it on a dead officer on a World War I battlefield. On exercises I carried the Smith & Wesson strapped to my leg in a holster to which was clipped a blackened commando knife. With my face also blackened, I looked quite frightening. Fortunately (for me) I never used these weapons in combat, and surrendered the revolver anonymously to the British police thirty years after the war, under an amnesty for the possession of illegal weapons. The most useful weapons in the jungle turned out to be grenades, the Bren gun and the Sten gun. You could fire the guns from the hip and fling the grenades from a prone position, which made you feel better, even if you didn't hit anybody.

While we were playing soldiers in the summer and autumn of 1940, the real war was being fought in the sky. Isolated by the army regimen, we knew little about it. Occasionally it came to our attention in the form of a stick of bombs dropped on nearby York or an urgent message for Private Body, a public school graduate who continually aggravated the corporal in charge of our barrack room by his lazy insouciance. Body had three brothers in the Air Force. During our four months at Strensall all his brothers were shot down. The war was being fought not only in the air, but on and under the ocean and in Britain's bombed cities. Post-Dunkirk in 1940 until D-Day in 1944, the infantry in Britain were relatively sheltered. Life was more strenuous than dangerous.

After four months of arms drill, marching, running, jumping, crawling, digging, those of us deemed to have made the grade were sent to Officer Cadet Training Units (OCTUs). Neil and I were sent to Dunbar on Scotland's east coast, where we had a further three months of intensive training, including map-reading, night manoeuvres and sleeping out in the Scottish winter weather – more or less what I had been doing for pleasure before I enlisted. My only problem was on the parade ground, where I fell foul of the sadistic Regimental Sergeant Major, who spent much of his time on parade shouting and scaring the hell out of everyone. There was one suicide for which he was blamed. My own little *contretemps* arose from the fact that at Strensall I had been taught the drill routines of the King's Own Yorkshire Light Infantry, who marched at 140 paces a minute and carried their rifles either at the trail or held firmly to their sides. Regular infantry regiments carried their rifles at the slope on their left shoulders. So my first response to the command, 'Slo-o-ope arms!' followed by, 'Prese-e-ent arms!' was hesitant and fumbled. I was dispatched with saliva-spraying, red-faced oaths to a one-man awkward squad. Neil, who had learned the conventional drills at his school, gave me a private lesson that evening.

It was a bad start, but it finished all right. I was graded 'B'. There were four grades – A, B, C and D. No one got an A, and there were three Bs. One of the Ds, a Welshman called John Thomas, was a friend of mine. Not a natural soldier, he was commissioned into the

Royal Army Service Corps. The next time I saw him after Dunbar was the day after the relief of Imphal in June 1944, when I led the battalion advance party to find billets. In one house I inspected, I found John having tea and cakes with a nurse. Everybody's war was different. One thing the army never claimed was logic. Success could lead to demotion and mistakes were not always a bar to promotion. Just before we embarked in April, 1942, our medical officer made sixteen men seriously ill by injecting them with petrol, because he picked the wrong bottle off the shelf. The next time I saw him he was a Lieutenant Colonel at Corps headquarters.

Before being commissioned, we were invited to choose three regiments to which we would prefer to be posted. As always, I consulted Neil and we listed the Queen's Own Cameron Highlanders as our first choice. Thus lighthearted decisions determine destiny. From Dunbar, we went to William Anderson & Sons, the regimental outfitters in Edinburgh, where we were fitted out with kilts, Sam Browne belts, Glengarrys and Balmorals (headgear), cap badges, brogues, garters with flashes, *skean-dhus* (stocking daggers), gaberdine jackets and greatcoats with regimental buttons – an outfit good for impressing the girls, but quite unsuitable for our ensuing war.

The Balmoral

Chapter Three

Regimental Life

There's many a man of the Cameron clan
That has followed his chief to the field
He has sworn to support him, or die by his side,
For a Cameron never can yield.

I hear the pibroch sounding, sounding
Deep o'er mountain and glen,
While light, springing footsteps are trampling the heath,
'Tis the march of the Cameron men
'Tis the march, 'tis the march
'Tis the march of the Cameron men.

Regimental march of the Queen's Own Cameron Highlanders

O N REPORTING TO THE CAMERON DEPOT in Inverness, I was interviewed by the adjutant, who observed that I was wearing underpants. 'A jock-strap,' I said 'for hygienic reasons.' 'Not customary,' he said, and posted me forthwith to the 1st Battalion, after pointing out that my kilt was wrongly pleated. It was not the warmest of welcomes.

Anyone who served as an officer in the Camerons and who has read James Kennaway's *Tunes of Glory* – or seen the film of the book featuring Alec Guinness – will have recognized some of the characters. It is difficult to convey to civilians the reverence of regular officers for their regiment, its history and its arcane rituals. The longer the roll of battle honours, the greater the loyalty. The stronger the belief of uniqueness, the more rigid the discipline forming the template that shapes a regiment's officers. A regiment can be compared to a monastic order. Between the world wars, the regiments of the British army maintained themselves as proud hierarchies as steadfastly as if Waterloo had been their most recent engagement.

Regimental loyalties should not be underrated. They are a major asset to morale, to competitive spirit, and the key to many victories. Those who rationalized the army in the second half of the 20th century by amalgamating regiments and changing their names underestimated the emotional impact of their reorganizations, especially on Highland regiments, each with its own tartan, its own music, its own customs stemming from ancient battles. The Cameron Highlanders, known as 'the 79th in line', were amalgamated first with their neighbouring rivals the Seaforths, and then both were amalgamated with the Gordons. To long-serving soldiers, some of whose fathers and grandfathers served in those regiments, these unions were forced conversions. The Regiment had been a way of life, and service to the Regiment a worthy life mission. Even temporary soldiers like me became imbued with a touchy loyalty to the Regiment's name and reputation.

The first nine months of World War II did little to change the rituals of regimental life. Then Dunkirk forced the creation of a new kind of army. The remnants of dozens of units had to be rebuilt rapidly with whatever recruits were available. At officer level, this resulted in three strata – regular officers released from the treadmill of peacetime soldiering and suddenly promoted; territorial army officers, mostly family men yanked suddenly from their careers into the business of war; and 'Emergency Commissioned Officers' (like Neil and me), most of whom had enlisted on the outbreak of war.

The other ranks were also stratified. The WOs and NCOs were professional soldiers, while the private soldiers were mainly conscripts, with a scattering of old regulars. Only about eighty of the original 1st Battalion of the Cameron Highlanders had returned to England after the Dunkirk wipe-out. As a result, in 1941 conscripts were from Yorkshire, Lancashire and the Lowlands of Scotland – cultures which differed from one another and from the Highlanders of the Lochaber country which had been the historical catchment area of the regiment. Yorkshire miners, Glasgow dockers, Lancashire mill workers – products of the industrial revolution – had no knowledge of the lives of Highland crofters, and vice versa. Draftees from England were eyed with suspicion in a Scottish regiment. The Regimental Records commented in July 1940 that the battalion had been 'astonishingly' augmented by two drafts of 'Englishmen'. Into this hurriedly assembled *mélange*, we wartime *ingénue* newly-commissioned second lieutenants were dropped.

★ ★ ★

The Camerons were stationed in Thorne, a Yorkshire mining town, when I reported for duty in March 1941. Officers had to find their own billets. On my first evening, I dropped into a pub and struck up a conversation with a man who said that he and his wife would be glad to put me up. He turned out to be the local mine-owner. I found myself in a luxurious bow-windowed guestroom, overlooking a well-tended garden, with a four-poster bed.

Emerging from my new quarters on my first morning, I observed a Major in Cameron uniform leaving the next-door house, a more modest establishment. I omitted to salute him. He gave me a sideways look. I learned later he was Major R M 'Daddy' Riach DSO, a regular officer, second-in-command of the battalion and a crusty character at the best of times. My unpopularity with him was aggravated a few evenings later when he found me asleep in his favourite chair in the officers' mess. Junior officers were supposed to rise to their feet when field officers (i.e. Major and above) entered the mess. Fortunately for my military career, Major Riach was posted away shortly afterwards.

Mess life was governed by unstated protocols which could be learned only by transgressing them. Once a week there was a 'mess night', when we dressed up. I learned to drink port and pass the decanter to the left. Neil, having gone to a public school, had a better sense of protocol than I did. As a grammar school boy, I was sensitive to any whiff of class. After dinner on mess nights, a piper would march round the table playing marches and laments and four subalterns would be ordered to dance a reel. Neil was always selected. He was a bonny dancer. One of the many fringe benefits of my army life was that officers were taught Highland dancing by the pipe major. The way in which this might forward the war effort was not revealed.

Allan Roy, Commander of C Company, to whom I reported, was a big, handsome, warm-hearted man and a hero to me before I met him, because I had seen him play rugby for Scotland in 1938. The Commanding Officer, Lieutenant Colonel Pat Hannay, appealed to me as a father figure, but was invalided out shortly after I arrived. His successor, Lieutenant Colonel R E Hickson (called either 'Skin' or 'Ethel' behind his back) was a prime example of over-promotion. His idea of dinner conversation was to ask for the salt to be passed.

Egalitarianism was encouraged only among those of the same rank. Neil and I stuck together, and gradually formed, if not a bond, at least a fellow-feeling with the other subalterns who were regarded by senior officers as a lower form of life. When off parade with a few drinks in them, the subalterns were quite capable of finding ways to demonstrate their independence. For example, at a dinner given by the Camerons where Major General John L Grover, General Officer Commanding the Division, was the guest of honour, someone had the bright idea of slipping into the cloakroom and removing the crossed-sword insignia from the General's greatcoat, leaving only one pip on each shoulder, thus making the General's coat indistinguishable from those of the second lieutenants. When the General was ready to leave, his aide-de-camp (ADC) could not find his coat. The subalterns suffered a 6.30 am drill parade under the Regimental Sergeant Major for that escapade.

The full lieutenants (two pips on each shoulder) and the captains (three pips) were mostly older (25–30) and had been in the Territorial Army. The regular officers (upper twenties, early thirties) were either captains or majors. Second in command to Skin Hickson was Major Angus J J 'Sporran Jock' Somerville-McAlester. Two other regulars were Major Angus Douglas and the Adjutant, Captain Niall Baird, son of Major General Baird, to whom he had been ADC in India before the war. These children of the army were not exactly hail-fellow-well-met. It took me some time to realize that, while appearing to be snobbish, they were basically shy and felt ill at ease with those who did not share their backgrounds. Among the younger captains were Donald Callander and Colin Hunter, who had both won Military Crosses in France. Lieutenant Fitzroy McLean, who was to become Churchill's parachuted envoy to Yugoslavia, and subsequently a Member of Parliament, a successful travel author and, in his later years, a hotelier on Loch Fyne, manifested himself briefly before departing on his hush-hush mission. Of the senior regulars, only Angus McAlester was to serve with the battalion until the end of the campaign in Burma. Another officer who had been in France and who served for the duration

23

was Frankie Maclauchlan, the padre (Presbyterian, of course, in a Scottish regiment), thought by some of the senior officers, because of his mild manners, to be insufficiently inspiring. Frankie was to prove them wrong. He was awarded a Military Cross and Bar at the end of the campaign.

The 2nd Division, consisting of the 4th, 5th and 6th Brigades, had been rebuilt from the depleted force which had returned from Dunkirk. The Camerons were one of the three battalions of the 5th Brigade. By the summer of 1941, the Division was battle-ready. But there were no battles to fight. We, and tens of thousands like us, spent weary days and nights on coastal defence, the need for which became negligible after the Germans invaded Russia in June 1941. The infantry in Britain became temporarily a spare wheel in the war machine, while the war was fought at sea and in the air. Europe was to remain an unassailable fortress until the Americans arrived. The only theatre where British troops were engaged was North Africa, for which we assumed we were being groomed. We could not know that within six months the Japanese attack on Pearl Harbour would be followed by their conquest of Malaya, the fall of Singapore and the invasion of Burma.

In August 1941 we moved from Thorne to Knaresborough, a more classy town, where training consisted of long route marches and night operations, the intention being that we would counter-attack if the Germans achieved a bridgehead. Officers were sent on 'courses'. After graduating successfully from a battle course at Lincoln, I was promoted to be Assistant Motor Transport Officer, an egregious mis-appointment. I couldn't even drive. But what an opportunity! Within six weeks I had been taught the wonders of the internal combustion engine and was driving everything – trucks, staff cars, lorries, even tanks. My favourite vehicle was the motor-cycle. I loved marshalling convoys. You roared ahead to a junction or crossroads, dismounted and signalled the convoy through, then remounted, overtook the convoy and repeated the drill. Dispatch riders were the cowboys of the army.

My education included a week's course on bomb disposal, when I began to learn about explosives. We toured bomb craters, were taught how to calculate the size of a bomb from the size of the crater, and how to identify UXBs (unexploded bombs), for the dismantling of which the Royal Engineers provided ice-nerved experts.

After the war I often reflected that the army gave me my first lessons in management. It was called leadership. You learned it on the job. A twenty-year-old ex-boy-scout would be made responsible for the care and feeding of a platoon of thirty men, who would touchingly trust him to take the right decisions in moments of stress. One's mentor was a platoon sergeant of senior years, whom a young officer could, should, and mostly did, consult before giving orders. Among lessons learned in the army which I later found relevant to corporate life were: stay close to those under your command; don't try to hide anything; and explain your reasoning when announcing a decision. It is unfortunate that the word leadership has been demoted by the jargon of management.

Above all, the army of the 1940s taught its young officers – or at least gave them the opportunity to learn – how to handle relationships within a hierarchy. Widely different personalities, flung together by the exigencies of war, had to live and work together. There was no question of compatibility. You could not resign, and nobody got fired. So we learned willy-nilly that most useful of management lessons – tolerance of others' shortcomings. We mastered the art of invisibly amending orders so that both discipline and common sense were served, an art highly relevant to the kind of warfare for which we were destined. While not regarded with enthusiasm by most people, jungle warfare provided more scope for self-reliance and individual initiative than did mechanized warfare. It forced interdependence, for which my egalitarian instincts were an unconscious preparation. From the start, while requiring that I be addressed as 'sir' on parade, I invited the Jocks to use my first name off parade. This was unusual.

Not only does the jungle make everyone equal – an above-average percentage of senior officers were killed or wounded in Burma – it introduces us to death, our sanction for submission to the dumb drills of war, more casually and more intimately than mass barrages or blanket bombing. Death in the jungle is something that happens to individuals before your eyes. They may be the enemy, they may be your comrades, and it could be you. It is the unexpected bullet.

Shortly after I joined the battalion in 1941, I met death for the first time in a personal way when my brother Tommy was killed in an air crash. It happened three weeks after his wedding to Evelyn Alice Tucker, a water-colour artist and scion of a prominent family. I had been his best man. Tommy, a rugby player of international class and a champion golfer, had embarked on a business career and awaited call-up as a conscript. He then chose the Royal Air Force and trained as a bomber pilot. His aircraft had inexplicably dived into a park in Leicester, close to where he and Evelyn were lodging. He had jumped, but his parachute failed to open.

Straight off a forty-eight-hour exercise, I was granted three days' compassionate leave. Evelyn, whom we found in bed hugging Tommy's pyjamas, was taken home by her parents. Tom and Marion, who had clung wordlessly to each other on the journey from Glasgow, were stern-faced and silent. Two senior air force officers saluted in unison when our returning train pulled out of Leicester station, whereupon Tom curled into the corner of the compartment and sobbed uncontrollably, beyond comfort. Late that night in Glasgow, Tom and I went to the station to meet the train carrying the coffin. 'He'll know we're here,' Tom said.

My role in the obsequies included an all-night vigil at the open coffin, my sister-in-law seriously believing that Tommy might rise again. After the funeral, she asked me to scatter his ashes at a remote spot in the hills where they had pledged themselves to each other on a summer's picnic.

I had read a lot about death. Now it was real. Sitting alone with Tommy's lifeless body, in what ironically was called our living room, I reflected that death is a tragedy only when it is premature and needless; that the heartache of parents for their dead children is an almost unbearable burden; and that the dead do not have much interest in funerals. Evelyn never remarried.

In December 1941, ominously on Pearl Harbour day, the 2nd Division was moved from Yorkshire to Oxfordshire, in preparation for embarkation overseas. We did not enjoy the new location. In Yorkshire the housewives would pass round jugs of tea when we halted during route marches. In Oxfordshire they pulled down the blinds lest we might see into their houses.

Neil got married to Phil, the girl of his dreams, in the church in picturesque Adderbury. With a friend of Phil's we had a foursome expedition to London, which included a visit to the Palladium Theatre, where I became part of the show by dancing in the aisle in my kilt with a chorus girl. The theme song of the show was *A Pretty Girl Is Like a Melody*. At the end of the show, two nondescript men, spotlighted alone on the vast stage, rocking gently in rhythm, sang softly to the rapt audience and were greeted with thunderous applause. It was Flanagan and Allen, the great double act of the 1930s' music halls, singing their theme song *Underneath the Arches*. Performing in blitzed and still blitz-prone London, those two guys, who had been so poor they really *had* slept underneath the arches, gave me and, I am sure, many other pre-embarkation soldiers, a heartwarming nugget among our stores of nostalgic memories. That which in peacetime we enjoy but take for granted becomes in wartime something to treasure.

During this period I was asked to lead my platoon on a recruiting march through Oxford, presumably to cheer up the civilian population. We were inspected by our Regimental Colonel-in-Chief King George VI, by Winston Churchill, and by the Colonel of the Regiment, Major General Neville Cameron.

On embarkation leave, having been jilted by Morris Cameron some months earlier (I was too young for her), I impetuously became engaged to a girl mellifluously named Maisie Dalrymple whom I had met in Greek class. Maisie wisely cancelled the arrangement some months later. Overseas service for the British Army in World War II was four years, an unreasonable time of separation even for mature relationships. There were to be many sad 'Dear John' letters before the Division's return in October 1945. I wonder what happened to Maisie, the policeman's daughter? By chance I did learn what happened to Morris Cameron. At a dinner in Glasgow in 1967 I was sitting next to Mrs Wotherspoon, a Campbeltown bookseller. I asked her if she had ever known Morris Cameron, daughter of the postmaster in Islay. 'Oh, yes,' she said. 'She became a teacher. She never married. She died three weeks ago.'

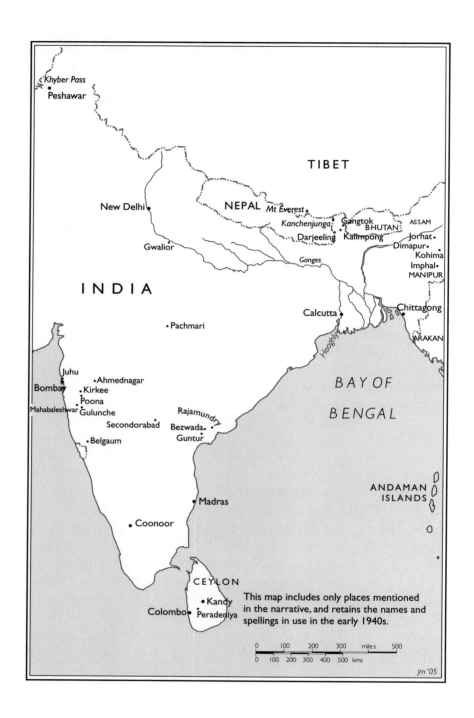

Khyber Pass
Peshawar

TIBET

New Delhi

NEPAL   Mt Everest
Kanchenjunga   Gangtok   BHUTAN   ASSAM
Darjeeling   Kalimpong   Jorhat
Gwalior   Dimapur
Kohima
Imphal
MANIPUR
Ganges

INDIA

Pachmari

Calcutta   Chittagong

Hooghly   ARAKAN

BAY OF
BENGAL

Juhu
Bombay   Ahmednagar
Kirkee
Poona
Mahabaleshwar   Gulunche
Rajamundry
Secondorabad   Bezwada
Guntur
Belgaum

ANDAMAN
ISLANDS

Madras

Coonoor

CEYLON   This map includes only places mentioned
Kandy   in the narrative, and retains the names and
Colombo   Peradeniya   spellings in use in the early 1940s.

0   100   200   300   miles   500

0   100   200   300   400   500   kms

jm '05

28

Chapter Four

Destination Unknown

I have not become the King's First
Minister in order to preside over the
liquidation of the British Empire.
WINSTON CHURCHILL, November 10, 1942

THE MARNIX VAN SIND ALDEGONDE, a Dutch cruise liner converted to a troopship, was quite comfortable for the officers –
six subalterns to a cabin – but Stygian for the troops who slept in
hammocks on the lower decks. We sailed from Liverpool on 11 April
1942. Ignoring rules of secrecy, a Jock whose home was in Liverpool had arranged that his wife would come to a top-floor tenement
window overlooking the dockside at an appointed hour when he
would be on the prow of the ship, so that they could wave to each
other.

As the first ships in the convoy moved past those still moored,
the troops lined the decks to cheer one another. Later that day a
destroyer circled us dashingly as the *Marnix*, with us swaying on
parade wearing life jackets, took its place in the convoy. The
destroyer commander offered, through his loudspeaker, to lead us
in community singing.

Nobody had told us where we were going, but we had been
issued with tropical clothing and assumed our destination was the
desert war in North Africa. We were part of a huge convoy which
sailed west and south and east and after eighteen days anchored off
Freetown in Sierra Leone. For most of us, this was our first glimpse
of any country other than our own. 'Look how green it is,' said one
Jock excitedly. We were not allowed to go ashore.

The convoy proceeded southward with a lighter escort, its task to
get us safely to Cape Town, a magical way-station and beacon of
hope to many thousands of British troops before and after us, five
weeks away from the blackout and austerity of their besieged
homeland. This, we said to ourselves, is what life will be like some

day. Cape Town's British-descended community was untiringly hospitable. Girls! There was said to be one ship in the convoy with nurses aboard ... it wasn't ours. It being a Sunday when we docked at Cape Town, I asked Skin Hickson's permission to go ashore to attend church service. He interrogated me suspiciously and gave me two hours' leave.

The following day we marched through the city behind our pipe band, and along the shore to Camps Bay. Scottish expatriates came to the gates of their cottages, tears flowing, some calling out greetings in Gaelic. Camps Bay had a personal meaning for me since my parents had been married there in 1914.

After camping for two days below Table Mountain we re-embarked. When we were off Madagascar, it was announced that we were headed, not for Egypt, but India. Nobody said why. Maybe 'they' had decided there were enough troops in the Middle East for the build-up to El Alamein; maybe they wanted us in reserve in case the Germans should break through to Iran from Russia; maybe they feared (the most likely presumption) that the Japanese, who were then completing their conquest of Burma, would invade India; maybe they feared that the Indian Army would not be able to cope with the Congress Party's threatened rebellion against British rule; maybe we were seen as a strategic replacement for the 18th Division, which had preceded us to Bombay by a few months, only to be shipped onwards to Singapore in time to be surrendered to the Japanese. Maybe all of these things. The diversion of our convoy was a tiny decision in the pattern of war, albeit one that changed the lives of 15,000 men.

The nine-week voyage in close confinement brought the junior officers of the Camerons into closer communion. Having no escape from one another's foibles, we became more tolerant of them. Sailing into the unknown deepened our sense of brotherhood. As the mess teetotaller, I was on late-night duty to waken those who fell asleep in their chairs, pipes drooping, and lead them gently to their cabins. In the tropics the Jocks slept on deck. The temperature on F deck one night was 45 degrees centigrade. We had deck sports, concerts, sing-songs and games. The *Marnix* – sunk, alas, in the Mediterranean in 1943 – was a floating home.

Bombay, however, was not welcoming. We lay in harbour in sweltering pre-monsoon heat for the first ten days of June. India Command had not expected us and no doubt regarded us as transients. A British division was more expensive to maintain than an Indian division. When we finally got ashore, we were entrained ninety miles up-country to Kirkee, near Poona, where we were invited to occupy eight-man tents in a muddy field in the dark, some of the Jocks discovering painfully what scorpions are. The rations were dehydrated potatoes, onions and bread.

Before leaving for Kirkee, we had been allowed a day in Bombay, where, wearing solar topees, khaki shirts and knee-length shorts with turn-ups designed, obviously by somebody who would never have to wear them, to be turned down in the evening to protect one's knees against mosquitoes, we looked ridiculous among the dhotis, saris and home-spun tropical suits. Bombay, like Cape Town, was untouched by war but had uneasy political undertones to which my first conversation with an Indian introduced me. As we walked up Pherozeshah Mehta Road from the docks, we stopped at a shop to leave my watch for repair. As we left, I asked the Sikh jeweller for directions to the nearest police station. 'Why,' he said, 'do you want to go to the police station?' I explained that Neil had a school friend who lived in Bombay and we hoped the police would help us to locate him. The Sikh regarded me sardonically. 'My friend,' he said, 'you will learn that the police in India are not here to help people. And neither are you.'

We did manage to locate Neil's friend, whose name was Mukhtar Munjee, the son of rich merchants living on Malabar Hill. He proved most hospitable, driving us at midnight to his shack on Juhu Beach. Neil and I had by this time teamed up with Vic Kilgour, another wartime volunteer who became a lifelong friend. Vic was witty, artistic, creative. We made a troublesome trio. Arriving back at our cabins at 5 am (reporting time being midnight), we found notes on our bunks to report to the adjutant. Paraded a few days later before a thin-lipped Skin Hickson, who questioned us separately in exhaustive detail, we were each sentenced to five days' orderly officer duties. This meant staying up all night in the orderly tent. Skin assumed we had been to a brothel, as had some of our brother officers. Instead we had been committing an offence more serious in his eyes – consorting with Indians.

A mile from our muddy field stood one of the symbols of 200 years of British rule – Government House of the State of Bombay. The Governor and his wife and daughters kindly invited the officers in groups to tea each day. Cucumber sandwiches served by turbaned bearers and small talk in a pillared drawing room were hard to relate to our boots newly cleansed of mud and our uniforms freshly starched for the occasion.

In August the Congress Party's rebellion against British rule broke out, and we were dispatched posthaste to Bezwada, Rajamundry and Guntur, South Indian towns where eight police and an unknown number of 'rioters' had been killed the night before we arrived. As we paraded with fixed bayonets to intimidate the populace, I remembered the Sikh jeweller's words. Innocents abroad, we found ourselves called on to defend an empire of which even the best informed of us at that time knew little. In the following three years, a few of us began to learn something about India and the teachings of Gandhi – *ahimsa* (non-violence) and *satyagraha* (passive resistance). To the Jocks, however, India was and remained an alien culture, an uninviting world lying outside the whitewashed stones demarcating our camp boundaries. Finding no friendly environment – no housewives with jugs of tea by the roadside – they withdrew into their cocoon of comradeship, the daily regimen and dreams of repatriation. When given day-passes, the Jocks were not allowed to go into the bazaars. They had to stay in the cantonments where cinemas, Chinese restaurants and brothels provided the only scope for relaxation. Scanning dismally the lengthy Chinese menus, they always ordered egg and chips.

We officers, however, found ourselves surprised and sometimes embarrassed beneficiaries of the privileges of British colonial life. In every town there was a 'Europeans Only' club of which we were automatically honorary members, Indians being admitted only as servants. I did not then worry about the Indians (although I should have) but about the Jocks. The clubs did not admit 'other ranks'. The same discrimination applied to life in the traditional barracks, of which we had a brief taste in Secunderabad after the Congress rebellion. The officers' mess quarters were spacious and comfortable; the Jocks slept in rows on charpoys (string beds).

The 'Europeans Only' rule could lead to some bizarre interpretations. Some in the Anglo-Indian community, who numbered about half a million at that time, could pass as Europeans while their siblings with darker complexions could not. Outside Bombay's Breach Candy swimming club I watched three sailors from a visiting American warship seeking entrance. One of them was stopped at the turnstile, the admissions clerk pointing to the 'Europeans Only' sign. He was a Nisei (Japanese American). The three of them talked together. The Nisei said, 'You guys go on in.' The look on his face as he turned away was a commentary on a crazy world. India in 1942 was not the environment for a people's war.

Although the Congress Party rebellion was quickly quashed, and Nehru, Gandhi and other leaders arrested, the 2nd Division was still kept as a reserve for 'internal security' against 'civil unrest', these being the euphemisms of the day. The Congress Party slogan was uncompromising: 'Quit India'. Although many of its followers were, under Gandhi's influence, committed to non-violence, there were 'criminal elements' who were not. We would assemble sometimes at midnight and, with a police guide, drive our trucks without lights across country to surround villages in which the police wished to interview suspicious characters. We would cordon the targeted village before dawn and intercept anyone who tried to sneak away. What we had not reckoned with was that many villagers went into the fields at dawn to do their morning business, so we had to make exceptions.

The police chief would assemble the villagers and address them. They would listen with distant, almost benevolent, interest. In one village I observed a young man, dressed in spotless white, who seemed amused by the whole affair. 'Who's he?' I asked the police chief. 'He's the one we want, but I've nothing on him!'

Our main occupation was to train for jungle warfare, an art in which the Japanese had taught the British and Indian armies some bitter lessons in Malaya and Burma. To operate in small groups, to be independent of roads, to be self-sufficient, to learn how to use the jungle as your friend, to be ready for close-quarter combat –

G (R) Platoon practising unarmed combat. Author on the right. *Inset* The bush hat.

these were the principal lessons. The Japanese had been aided in these tactics by their ability to live off the land. There was little hope of training British troops to emulate them. We had to devise answers of our own. One of those was to be supplied by airdrops, but in 1942 that was a long way off.

A step towards the mastery of the new kind of warfare was the formation of a 'Guerrilla (Reconnaissance) Platoon' in each battalion. By kind providence I was given command of the Camerons' G (R) Platoon – given, in effect, freedom to live rough in the Indian countryside with fifteen men of my choosing. One of the first things I did was to discard their solar topees and rig them out in bush hats, which I found in the quartermaster's store. This sensible headgear of Australian origin was soon adopted throughout the Division. In the adventures of the G (R) Platoon was born my love for India, which was to be my home for ten years after the war.

In preparation for my new role I was sent on a course on jungle warfare in Upper Assam. It was so badly run that I wrote an adverse report, after which the school was closed. Even so, meeting the other 'students' did more for everyone's education than even a well-run course could have accomplished. At this school I met my first American, a marvellously muscular sergeant. The camp was not far from the River Teesta where it emerges from the Himalayas with glacially green rushing waters. On a bet, my American friend and I flung ourselves into the river and finished up a mile down-stream, breathless and invigorated. I find it sad in retrospect that British and American troops never fought side by side in Burma, as they did in Europe. We had no contact with General Stilwell's forces who in 1944 brilliantly captured the airfield at Myitkyina in Northern Burma. The only Americans we met in Burma were US air crews who, in partnership with the Royal Air Force, ferried us in and out of Burma in 1944 and 1945.

At the Assam jungle school I also got to know my first Indians and began to perceive how their thought processes differed from mine. For example, near the end of a two-day trek, I decided the time had come to slice up a large pineapple which I had carried attached to my belt. Everyone took his slice with gratitude except two Indian officers who accepted their portions in silence. I was offended. I should not have been. Gratitude is a Christian concept. According to Hindu philosophy, the giver confers benefit on himself.

The (G) R platoon learned to live off the land, which meant buy-ing chickens, eggs and rice in the villages. The villagers saw us as a kind of travelling show and gathered round our campsites. British city boys who had joined up to fight the Germans, we found our-selves dropped, like space travellers, into an exotic but friendly society where we could communicate only in sign language. Ever since these days, I have urged friends visiting India not to judge it by its cities or tourist spots. In the villages nobody begged, because poverty had little meaning where everyone, except the *bania* (money lender) and the *zamindar* (landowner), was at the same level of subsistence. We learned to use dried cow-dung as fuel and to make *chapattis* (flour pancakes) in our mess tins.

Long after the war, I spoke with a social worker whose job was to go round Indian villages propagating birth control. He told me how he had once squatted with a toil-worn farmer, father of many chil-dren, explaining the virtues and mechanics of contraception. At the end of his homily he asked the villager if he was now willing to limit his parenthood. The villager asked him: 'What else is there?' The social worker had no answer.

Once we camped for a week in the grounds of a Methodist mission learning rural crafts, including how to make sandals out of sisal fibre. Observing that the mission was a bustling social centre, I asked Ms Lillian Picken, who had been there for twenty-nine years, how many converts to Christianity she had made. Her answer – 'one' – took me totally by surprise. Most of her converts to Christianity, she felt, had been superficial. Yet she did not feel unfulfilled, seeing example as more important than precept. The mission was concerned more with teaching self-help than with doctrine.

Hinduism has a way of absorbing other creeds. Converted lower caste Hindus, attracted by the egalitarianism of Christianity, still regarded themselves, and were regarded by the upper castes, as untouchables. Gandhi called them *harijan* (the chosen of God), but even he could not change deeply ingrained prejudices and was to be assassinated by an extremist Hindu a few years later. Travelling in South India after the war, I noticed that communism had its greatest appeal in areas where the majority of people were officially Christians.

During these days of jungle training, when we could disappear for a week or ten days at a time, we were benefiting from the law of unintended consequences. If the Japanese had not forced their enemies to explore new techniques of warfare, we in the G (R) Platoon would never have escaped the dreary drills that fill the days of army camps. After the war, when I was working on *The Times of India*, I wrote an article called 'An opportunity missed', lamenting the fact that thousands of British troops were embarking for home as ignorant of India as the day they arrived. The editor turned it down. 'Too sensitive,' he said.

★ ★ ★

Bombay was blessedly within reach from the various rural camps we occupied in Western India in 1942 and early 1943. On my first weekend there I met Peggy Milne, daughter of Sandy Milne, a Scottish engineer who had emigrated to Japan via the trans-Siberian Railway in 1912 and had spent his life in Asia working for an oil company. He had met Peggy's mother, also Scottish, when she was working as a nurse in India. Peggy, born in Calcutta, and her sister Kitty, born in Surabaya, had received, in the colonial tradition, their secondary and college education in England, from which they returned to India each summer. The war had prevented

their returning to the UK in 1939. Neil, Vic and I became regular visitors to the Milnes' penthouse apartment overlooking the Cricket Club of India.

Peggy and I, both twenty-two years old, were soon in love and decided to get married right away. This involved my getting permission from Skin Hickson, who advised me against haste, pointing out that he and his wife had been engaged for seven years. He had already summoned me back from a vacation with the Milnes, not for any military emergency, but because my identity card had been stolen. This caused me to apply for a transfer, which was denied. Skin and I were not exactly pals.

Our wedding took place in the Scots Kirk in Bombay on June 2, 1943, exactly twenty-nine years after my parents' wedding in Cape Town. The uncertainty of war lends clarity and urgency to great life-decisions. We honeymooned in Darjeeling, Kalimpong and Gangtok in Sikkim, trekking up to the Tibetan border, living in remote dak bungalows with exotic names like *Rississum*. We were entertained by the Maharaja of Sikkim and met the royal family of Bhutan. Views of Kanchenjunga and Everest, orchids, butterflies, giant land crabs, leeches … war could not have seemed further away.

Yet it was closer than we knew. One of our sister brigades had been dispatched to the Arakan, where it had fought valiantly in a disastrous campaign and had had severe casualties, losing its brigadier when its headquarters was overrun. Unbelievably, at my level, no lessons were passed on from this defeat. At this time, great battles were being fought in North Africa, in Russia and in the Pacific. In Britain a vast army was being prepared for the Second Front. We were in limbo. I grew impatient again. When the 1943 Wingate expedition behind Japanese lines in Burma became public, I again applied for a transfer and was again refused. We were being reserved, it was hinted, for something bigger.

Morale among the Cameron officers improved in May 1943 when Skin Hickson was removed from command. Angus McAlester took over *pro tem* until September, when we received a new Commanding Officer, Lieutenant Colonel Peter 'Raja' Saunders, another regular officer. That the Camerons remained a close-knit community and battle-ready to the point of staleness was mainly due to the company commanders – Allan Roy, Colin Hunter, David Graham and Dave Davidson, all with the rank of Captain. The subalterns, warrant officers and non-commissioned officers provided the backbone of what had become a brotherhood – a remarkable moulding of unity from diversity.

Talk of 'plans', always secret, continued. Suddenly our training was switched from jungle warfare to combined operations, i.e. invasion by sea. We guessed that this could be attributed to the creation of South East Asia Command under Lord Louis Mountbatten, who had previously been in charge of combined operations in the UK. He lost no time in transferring his headquarters from Delhi to Kandy in Ceylon, which suggested that he did not see his immediate goal as merely the recapture of Burma. From subsequent reading of history, I learned that at Cairo in 1943, Churchill had promised Chiang Kai-Shek that the Andaman Islands would be recaptured forthwith. The 2nd Division was earmarked for this. Allan Roy told me at one stage of the role my platoon was to play in this operation. There was only one snag: no landing craft were available. They were all needed for Sicily, then Italy, then for the invasion of France.

The 2nd Division was a strategic orphan, reserved for emergencies, denied supplies that would enable it to mount an offensive. Plans were drawn up and cancelled for more than one amphibious operation, including one of Churchill's wilder ideas – the seizure of the northern tip of Sumatra.

Seldom can so much intensive training have been done to so little purpose. Reading about Stalingrad, Anzio, Tarawa, New Guinea, I felt frustrated, even guilty. We did not know that our frustration was shared at high levels, notoriously by the eccentric Orde Wingate who, undeterred by his unpopularity with India Command, was preparing with the personal blessing of Churchill to mount a second, much bigger, expedition behind Japanese lines in Burma. Even more frustrated was General 'Vinegar' Joe Stilwell, at loggerheads with everyone. He was threatening to go it alone in North Burma and re-open the land route to China with American and Chinese troops.

Our switch to combined operations had a delightful fringe benefit – encampment on Juhu Beach, sixteen miles north of Bombay for several weeks. First came two weeks on the shores of a mountain-girt reservoir called Khadakvasla, where we swam and ran and climbed. Sailing across the lake one day, I ordered my entire platoon overboard without warning, complete with boots, clothes, helmets and rifles. The idea was to simulate an emergency. We all made it to shore – just.

As a parting flourish to our living-off-the-land, I marched my platoon to Juhu from Ahmednagar, 170 miles across the Western Ghats, where we encountered aboriginal tribes as strange to us as we were to them. At Juhu, we practised swimming while wearing boots and helmets and carrying our rifles. Once, cut off by the incoming tide, my batman, Stan Mawdesley – a superb athlete – and I decided to swim across a tidal creek to avoid a five-mile walk. Arriving at the opposite shore, I thought I'd lost Stan, strong swimmer though he was. I saw his hat floating in the muddy rushing current. But the hat was moving shoreward, with Stan underneath it. He had a great pair of lungs.

After some weeks of combined operations training, which included embarking on a troopship on one side of Bombay harbour and disembarking at the other, we returned to yet another tented camp, where the G (R) Platoon relieved its boredom by experimenting with booby traps and explosives. Demonstrating these to a sceptical audience, I blew myself up with a pound of guncotton, and spoke in an unnaturally loud voice for the next few days. On another occasion, we wanted to find out how big a crater we could make to block a road. After planting the recommended amount of explosives, we added a few spare mortar bombs and retreated rapidly. But not far enough. Clods of earth rained down not only on us, but on a nearby football match, which was abandoned. One clod went through the roof of the cookhouse of a neighbouring battalion and landed in the soup. As indeed, did I. I was sent to apologize.

Boxing was added to football and cross-country runs. Sergeant Major Tommy Cook, ex-army boxing champion, undertook to teach me by inviting me to hit him as hard and as often as I liked. He didn't even notice it. The events of each day consisted of reveille, inspections, exercise, parades, meals, mail and lights-out. In the officers' mess tent after dinner, the hours were filled with drinking, playing cards and occasionally playing pranks. For example, Neil told Bobby Sherwood, an assiduous womanizer, about his beautiful sister in Canada. Bobby wrote to her saying how lonely he was. After some weeks, there was an affectionate letter from Canada, which he shared with us ecstatically. It was indeed a lovely letter. I know, because I had written it, just happening to have a Canadian stamp on which I had carefully sketched the postmark. We decided not to tell Bobby.

During the monsoon in 1943 we had a climatically pleasant interlude in the jungle near Mahableshwar, a hill-station in the Western Ghats, the range of hills about 2,000 feet above sea level demarcating the western escarpment of the Deccan Plateau, and were then allocated yet another barren hillside at Gulunche, about fifty miles south of Poona. As time dragged on, Cameron officers who had connections began to drift away. Pat McLean, a lawyer from Edinburgh who had joined the battalion on the same day as me, was seconded to a legal department in Delhi because he was considered too old for active service; Roy McKelvie, a newspaperman, went into Public Relations; Donald Callander was shipped home with a tropical ulcer on his leg; Ian Stewart, a jazz pianist who had been leader of the Savoy Orpheans, became a Brigade Major. After a business dinner in a private room at the Savoy in 1982, I popped my head into the main dining room and observed a white-haired figure at the piano. The headwaiter confirmed that it was Ian. He used to give jazz renderings of *The March of the Cameron Men* whenever we got near a piano.

Incredibly, in March 1944, the Division was ordered to relax 'after your hard training', have some leave and come back ready for the big push – when landing craft would be available. I believe the Division would have continued to be the victim of a divided – indeed quarrelsome – high command and a low priority theatre starved of supplies if *force majeure* had not intervened.

Early in March, I had been posted to a 'Combined Operations Training Centre' as an instructor. It was run by two lieutenant colonels, transferred from Italy to train the Indian Army in sea-borne landings. The absence of landing craft did not faze these chair-borne planners. One hundred miles from the ocean, on the arid plains of the Deccan Plateau, Gurkhas, Punjabis and other Indian soldiers were taught to crouch in mock-up landing craft and charge up imaginary beaches marked with tape. The high command's intention was to by-pass the Arakan stalemate and make coastal and island landings behind the Japanese, as the Americans were doing in the Pacific, thus avoiding the fearsome challenge of fighting across the jungle-covered north-south mountain ranges of Assam and Manipur into the plains of Burma. Under this plan, Stilwell and Wingate, whose second airborne expedition into Central Burma was about to take off, would look after the northern front. The existing forces in Imphal, Kohima, Dimapur and Arakan would secure the defence of the borders of India. We, the 2nd Division, would be storming ashore somewhere in the Bay of Bengal.

General Mutaguchi, commanding the Japanese 15th Army in Burma, had other ideas. Towards the end of March, he unleashed three divisions across the River Chindwin to infiltrate through the roadless hills of Assam and Manipur with the aim of capturing first Imphal and Kohima and then Dimapur, which was the main supply depot for the whole Central Burma front. Suddenly, the 2nd Division, scattered over thousands of miles of Western and Southern India, with many on leave, or, like me, on detachment, was ordered to rush to Dimapur, 2,000 miles away. The Camerons at this time were in Ahmednagar, sixty miles north of Poona. On March 24 they set out by road and rail for Dimapur, where they arrived on April 2.

These events were not publicly announced. Censorship ensured that the Japanese invasion was not reported. When a movement order for me to rejoin my battalion was received, my bosses saw it as routine, and requested I stay with the Combined Operations Training Centre, which, they assured me, would be at the heart of the planned sea-borne operations. Finally, a top-priority order came through and I was released. This had one advantage: I could fly into battle – from Bombay to Calcutta by Blenheim Bomber, and from Calcutta to Imphal and then on to Jorhat by Dakota transport. Also on that flight was Brigadier Warren, Commander of the 161st Brigade, which included the 4th battalion of the Royal West Kents who had heroically withstood the Japanese onslaught on Kohima before the 2nd Division arrived.

I reached Jorhat twenty-four hours after leaving Bombay and thumbed a lift to the 2nd Division's rear headquarters in Dimapur, where I read with disbelief the casualty list of the Camerons since they had gone into action. The following morning, a truck dropped me at Zubza, the site of the Camerons' first battle. I shouldered my pack and Sten gun and looked 1,500 feet upwards at the misty, jagged skyline. As I clambered up the hill in a mixed file of Jocks and Nagas, whose loyal and voluntary help in evacuating casualties and portering supplies was an acknowledged, but never measured, factor in the Kohima battle, a Japanese plane swooped over the ridge and blew up an ammunition dump, causing us to bury our faces in the mud.

At last, nearly four years after becoming a soldier, I had found the action.

Chapter Five

Into Battle

With reference to the narrative of events, far from permitting myself to derive it from the first source that came to hand, I did not even trust my own impressions, but it rests partly on what I saw myself, partly on what others saw for me, the accuracy of the report being always tried by the most severe and detailed tests possible.
THUCYDIDES *History of the Peloponnesian War*

KOHIMA STANDS ON A RIDGE among jungle-clad hills, 5,000 feet and forty-two twisty miles above Dimapur, the railhead and supply base which lies on the eastern fringe of the wide, flat fertile valley of the Brahmaputra. One hundred roadless miles to the east the hills run down from the border with Burma to the River Chindwin, across which, at the beginning of March 1944, General Katuko Sato's 31st Division had set out on their 'March to Delhi', hoping to live on the rice they could carry, provisions they could buy or seize from Naga villagers and the oxen that they drove before them. They had reached Kohima without serious challenge except for a fierce battle with the 50th Indian Parachute Brigade at Sangshak, which dearly bought time for the defenders of Kohima. The Kohima garrison, manning the ridge round which the road from Dimapur curls towards Imphal, consisted of battalions of the Assam Regiment and the Royal West Kents. Vastly outnumbered, they fought stubbornly, suffered severe losses and held out until relieved by the 2nd Division, summoned from its bases 2,000 miles away at such short notice as to suggest at least lack of foresight and at worst a degree of panic on the part of the 14th Army command.

Beginning to run out of steam, the Japanese decided to secure Kohima before advancing to Dimapur, the capture of which would have given them all the supplies they needed. Thus, overstretched invaders and hastily mustered defenders collided at a place so constricted by its terrain and so crucial to the overall Burma Campaign as to make close-quarter combat inevitable. There was no scope for open warfare or tactical retreat. Both sides were under do-or-die orders.

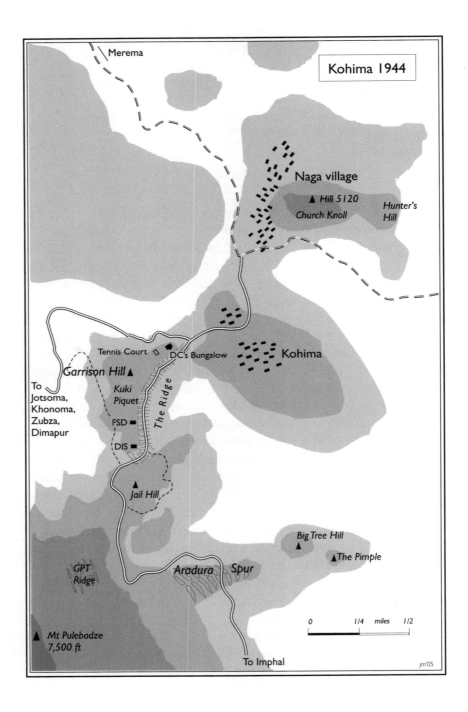

Merema

Kohima 1944

Naga village

▲ Hill 5120
Church Knoll

Hunter's
Hill

Tennis Court
DC's Bungalow
Kohima

Garrison Hill ▲

To
Jotsoma,
Khonoma,
Zubza,
Dimapur

Kuki
Piquet

The Ridge

FSD ■

DIS ■

▲
Jail Hill

Big Tree Hill
▲
▲The Pimple

GPT
Ridge

Aradura Spur

0   1/4   miles   1/2

▲ Mt Pulebadze
7,500 ft

To Imphal

jm'05

44

This head-on battle was also a clash between two cultures profoundly ignorant of each other. Both came from island nations off the coasts of continental land masses – geographies which had shaped their histories. The British represented a nation seeking to restore a fading empire, the Japanese a nation seeking to secure a new one. The Japanese, remembering Singapore and their conquest of Burma, underestimated their opponents; the British, remembering the same events, overestimated the battlefield prowess of their antagonists. Japanese conscripts mainly from rural areas, instilled with mindless readiness to die, were pitted against British counterparts mainly recruited from towns and cities, who had joined up to defend their home islands against the Germans.

If Thomas Hobbes had been writing *Leviathan* 300 years later than he did, he would have cited Kohima as an illustration of his theory of perpetual conflict between nations. Buried beneath the stark simplicity of conflict and the driving forces of duty, discipline and loyalty on both sides lurked the question: 'What the hell are we doing here?' Of the 30,000 men involved, nearly half, mostly Japanese, were to die.

When I arrived, the battle had been going for five weeks. The Camerons were on '5120', marking the feet above sea level of the hilltop on which lay Naga Village, overlooking the town and the ridge. They had established themselves there a few days before my arrival with a brilliantly executed night infiltration, scouted by Neil White. It was the Camerons' second major encounter. Earlier they had won the Division's first set-piece battle at Zubza, thirty-four miles from Dimapur, which cleared the road for the relief of the Kohima garrison. Zubza had cost the Camerons three dead and seventeen wounded, and the Japanese seventy-six dead.

The battle for Hill 5120 was chaotic. Silently by night the Camerons had reached a small bump on the north side of the village (later known as Hunter's Hill) and attempted to form a defensive box. However, because of the houses, they had not been able to dig in. Sniper fire caused many casualties. Then the Japanese counterattacked. The second night, the Camerons were forced to fall back past another small hill called Church Knoll to the western brow of 5120, where they were now entrenched. So were the Japanese, about 100 yards away. Around them and us were the ruins and debris of what had been Naga Village. To our right and below us, we could glimpse Garrison Hill, its few remaining trees denuded of branches, some bedraggled by shredded parachutes, thrusting starkly above the battlefield mud.

Hill 5120 was the left hook of General Grover's divisional battle plan, assigned to the 5th Brigade. The 4th Brigade was in the centre on the Kohima Ridge, commanding the road, and there was a right-hand outflanking movement by the 6th Brigade, also involving parlous night infiltrations. The Camerons had already lost eighty men killed and a like number wounded.

I reported to Angus McAlester at Battalion HQ, located in a hollow below the brow of the hill. He had that very day taken over as Commanding Officer, Peter Saunders having been given temporary command of a neighbouring brigade whose brigadier had been killed. I chatted with Allan Roy, who was commanding the HQ Company. 'What's it been like, Allan?' 'Can't think of one good thing about it,' he said. I asked Angus if I could take over what was left of my old platoon, but was ordered to be second-in-command of D Company, where Colin Hunter was the only surviving officer.

Colin, a soft-spoken, charming man gave me a rundown on events to date, as we crouched in his dugout. D Company had been the lead in the night assault on Naga Village, which initially had taken the Japanese by surprise. Everyone had worn tennis shoes. Their boots, when brought up to the line, had been delivered in a jumbled heap, so not everyone was wearing his own. There was pressure on the Brigade to recapture Church Knoll and Hunter's Hill. A company of Worcesters tried to take Church Knoll on the evening of my arrival, and I watched them being grenaded from foxholes and shelled by Japanese guns, firing on their own positions, confident that their troops were dug in deeply enough to be safe. The Japanese were better in defence than attack, when they tended to charge recklessly. In defence they were clever moles and frequently surprised their attackers by surviving heavy bombardments. I watched Church Knoll being strafed by RAF Hurribombers which, alarmingly, released their bombs far behind us.

The morning after my arrival, I was ordered to take a patrol to the north to seek a way round. The purpose of such patrols, under-taken by small groups who were used to working together, was to see and not be seen. The best timetable was to leave at dusk and work your way slowly, not to say quietly, into a hideout with a view and then wait until dawn. You then observed as much as you could of the enemy positions and made your way back by opportunity. If you reported that a route was feasible for attack, then came the hard part. You would be asked to guide the leading company. If the attack route was not feasible, artillery fire would be called on the enemy positions you had located. On some occasions, a Forward Observation Officer (FOO) from the Gunners would accompany a patrol and call for fire by radio.

The Jocks with whom I had practised jungle warfare were mostly dead or wounded. Three of the survivors, including Toorie McDonald, a big, soft-spoken crofter from Skye, agreed to come along. Although cover was scarce in the immediate vicinity of the village, all went well to begin with. We saw enough Japanese to suggest that the route was not feasible. On the way back, we came on four dead Camerons crumpled together on the ground. 'Get their discs,' I said to Toorie. While he was doing this, a Japanese patrol arrived and opened fire. Toorie got a bullet through the foot. This provided more evidence against the route. We scrambled back to the battalion's perimeter under cover of Bren gun fire.

Looking at the corpses we found on this patrol – the first battle casualties I had seen – I felt surprisingly impersonal. Friends of mine had inhabited these bodies until a few days before, but when death is not sanitized by funeral rites, you feel intuitively that the people are still around. Death is casual. Joe Christian, Neil White's batman, told me that a fellow next to him just bowed his head and died. He who dies from the unexpected bullet is expecting to live until the last second. Death in artillery fire or from aerial bombard-ment is different, being preceded by fear.

I reported to the newly-appointed Brigade Commander, Mike West, whose predecessor, Victor Hawkins, had taken a bullet in the crutch a few days earlier. (The fact that four brigadiers were killed or wounded at Kohima attests to the peculiar intimacy of the fighting.) Mike West, bare-chested and bush-hatted, interrupted my report to point out that I had not set the safety catch on my Sten gun, which, if you dropped it, could loose a burst. There are many ways of dying on a battlefield.

We were not bothered with bombardments. We heavily out-gunned the Japanese, who had been able to bring only mule-borne mountain guns over the hills. This was one reason why Mutaguchi lost his gamble at Kohima. Our gunners' twenty-five pounders were devastating and mostly accurate, although their shells were rationed throughout the battle.

Life for the individual soldier at Kohima was restrictive, to say the least. You are wakened by a shake, while it is still dark. You do not sit up, because the roof of the foxhole is only two feet from the floor. Instead, you slide forward to your stand-to post, where the floor has been deepened. The others are doing the same, pushing aside the sodden blanket they have been sharing. One is already awake, as he was the last on sentry duty – two hours on and four off.

Equipment on, rifle or automatic in hand, grenades ready, all are now staring out into the blackness. In fifteen minutes it will be first light, and in fifteen minutes more, there will be light enough to see, so that you can stand down – unless the mist fails to clear. All being well, you can now rely again on a single sentry. It is about quarter past five in the morning.

No one gets out of his foxhole, cramped and hurriedly dug though it may be. Foxholes are both inter-supporting and indepen-dent. You don't go visiting, and perching over the toilet hole is best done at night. You 'brew up' in the foxhole, with the aid of a petrol-burning cooker.

You are still eating yesterday's rations – bully beef, biscuits, cheese, milk, sugar and tea, which are issued in twenty-four hour packages along with a vitamin tablet, ten cigarettes and six sheets of toilet paper. Tea is the mainstay. Water supply may be all too sim-ple, but sometimes water is part of the ration supply. You become adept at achieving a drink, cleaning your teeth, shaving and wash-ing from a half mess-tin of water. But you can fill it again in thirty seconds if it's raining.

Some days you move – forwards, backwards, or sideways as ordered – carrying your rifle or automatic, 100 rounds of ammunition, and two or three grenades stuck in your belt. Each section's Bren gun is carried by turns, with the loaded magazines distributed. Also slung on your belt are bayonet, water bottle and mess tin. Your pack contains your pullover, soap, towel, socks, razor, mug, sterilizing tablets and anti-malarial cream. The monsoon cape is rolled on your belt. And almost as important as your weapon is your entrenching tool, digging being your daily exercise.

Action in jungle warfare requires a drastic change in values. A quick eye, a kindly act, a drink of water, a smile, an hour to sleep, a piece of dry ground – these rate far higher than at other times or in other places.

The Japanese, I reflected during my first days, were an ideal enemy because they were easy to hate. The little we knew about them was inaccurate. The booklets on *Know Your Enemy* told only about their uniforms and their weapons, not about their mentalities. Atrocity reports revealed them as inhuman and in the heat of battle we regarded them as sub-human. Yet they were excellent soldiers, courageous and self-sufficient, and they were experienced in combat, which we were not. They deserved better support from their high command. Mike West called them first class soldiers in a third class army.

No matter how dedicated we were, we could never match the fanaticism of Emperor worship. British troops could not even match the motivation of our comrades in the Indian Army, all professionals, all volunteers, organized under British officers into homogeneous battalions, and defending their homeland. The British troops' courage in the Burma Campaign was self-generated. Fed up and far from home, dropped by the chances of war into hardship and danger, they drew their strength from that sense of duty which, in times of peace, made them good citizens and family men.

Fifty-six years after the battle, at the annual reunion of Kohima veterans in York, I was approached by a man seeking to write his PhD thesis on what motivated British soldiers to fight in Burma. I said he could approach his subject under four headings: innate decency, discipline, pride of regiment and comradeship. Of these qualities, men like Arthur Woodall, Bill Cavanagh and Robert Moore-Hemsley, all killed before I got to Kohima, were prime exemplars. The first two were sergeants in my platoon, solid Yorkshire stock from the small towns in the triangle between Leeds, York and Bradford. Moore-Hemsley was a gentleman ranker. They were all older than me. We were friends.

After the battle at Zubza, the G (R) Platoon had located a large concentration of Japanese and brought down gunfire through their accompanying FOO. One of our guns fired short. Woodall and Cavanagh were killed immediately; Moore-Hemsley died of his wounds.

Moore-Hemsley was an Adonis-like, lion-hearted charmer. He once advised me that the most important thing in life was to 'find a good woman and give her a child'. Forty years after the battle, I happened to write a letter of complaint to an airline and received an answer signed by 'P Moore-Hemsley'. In my reply, I asked if his father had been in the Burma Campaign. He had. Phil Moore-Hemsley and I became friends and I was able to tell him about the father whom he had never seen. When he read this chapter in manuscript he learned for the first time of the manner of his father's death. We agreed he should not tell his mother.

Woodall, Cavanagh and Moore-Hemsley were three among tens of thousands killed in a little-publicized campaign which lasted four years; in which a dozen nations were engaged; in which both sides won victory and suffered defeat; and in a cause in which the inhabitants of the country over which it was fought (except for the Nagas and other hill tribes) did not feel involved. These are the inscriptions on their gravestones in the cemetery on Kohima Ridge:

Lance Corporal Robert Moore-Hemsley
In the garden of remembrance we meet every day.
Loving wife and son Philip.

Lance Sergeant Arthur Woodall
Still loved and missed. He is ever dear.
Though absent he is ever near. Phyllis.

Lance Sergeant William Cavanagh
A smiling face, a heart of gold
Memories of him will never grow old.

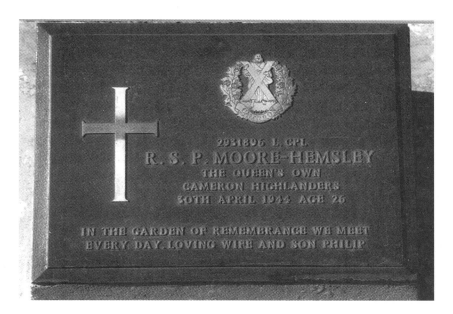

Amid the mechanics of warfare, we have no time to look for meaning. I remember abstractedly pocketing the first letter I received on 5120, which was from my mother informing me of my father's death. The death certificate said emphysema, but my brother Tommy's death had taken the heart out of him, and the privations of wartime life, including Home Guard sentry duty on winter nights, had added their toll. A quiet, self-effacing man who enjoyed simple pleasures, Tom was only sixty-one when he died. I never heard anyone speak ill of him, than which there are few better epitaphs. Marion for the rest of her life expressed gratitude for 'having shared thirty years of a good man's life'.

Life expectancy in Kohima at that time was statistically low. Yet everyone felt impervious. Death was always a surprise, followed by a flash of survivor's guilt. Woodall, Cavanagh and Moore-Hemsley, along with 1,400 others at Kohima, have graves, but the bodies of many, like that of Company Sergeant Major Tommy Cook, were never found. An archetypal warrior, Tommy had won a Distinguished Conduct Medal at Zubza by relieving a Japanese officer of his sword and using it to slaughter the owner and a few others. One who saw Tommy die on 5120 told me that he was bobbing up and down looking for targets when a sniper shot him through the eye. He was someone who seemed not to know fear, but of course he did. We all did. The trick was to convert it into controlled aggression, which manifested itself as a kind of dour fatalism. Fifty-eight years after the battle, a Naga expressed his admiration to Robert May, my son-in-law, for the way in which British troops moved to fill gaps caused by their dead and wounded.

There are ninety-three names on the Cameron memorial in Naga Village, but only sixty-four Cameron graves. The others were never found or their remains rest under the 'Known to God' stones, of which there are 134. While there were witnesses to Tommy Cook's death, some of the missing, like Dougal Cross and his batman, just disappeared. And sometimes the missing reappeared. Two Jocks in B Company, as noted in Company Sergeant Major Geordie Kerr's roll-book, went missing on May 6 and turned up again two days later explaining they had been captured in the middle of the night, escaped and made their way back to divisional headquarters, where they collected two new rifles and were now reporting back for duty.

The battle of 5120 was a moment of truth for the Camerons. The attack on Zubza had been a heady success. 5120 was chaos at all levels. D Company had been isolated and disorganized. Johnnie McNaught, the Intelligence Officer (who would have written a fine book on the campaign had he survived) was one of four killed when the Japanese shelled a house in which he had been ordered, under protest, to establish his section. Among other officers killed were Angus McKay, a scholarly, short-sighted fellow quite unsuited to the infantry; Arthur Carbonnel, who had distinguished himself by confronting and killing a Japanese sergeant major in whose satchel were important intelligence documents, died of gangrene in a field hospital; and Willie Macmillan, who was shot in the dark by some-one at our own Brigade headquarters. His last words were, 'Stop that bloody firing!' David Graham, awarded the MC for leading the attack on Zubza, was wounded and never returned to service. Also severely wounded was Johnnie Bain, who did return, only to be killed by machine-gun fire in his assault boat at the crossing of the Irrawaddy in 1945.

Bitter though the fighting was on 5120, there was heavier slaughter on the Kohima Ridge, where four battalions of the Division fought off repeated Japanese attacks and captured ground foot by foot. The battle for the tennis court in the grounds of the Commissioner's bungalow became a symbol of the intimacy of the combat on the Ridge.

The determination of the Japanese attacks bore witness to the courage of their soldiers and also to the fact that they were ruthlessly exploited by the ambitions of their high command. The Japanese were stuck at the end of a long, tenuous supply line, short of food, short of ammunition and with little air and artillery support. Their casualties at Kohima were such that after a month of fighting they simply did not have enough men to hold their positions. Their Commander, General Sato, sought permission to retreat, which was not granted. He gave the order anyway, and was later sacked.

The fragility of the Japanese supply chain was illustrated to me forty years after the battle by Masao Hirakubo, who, after working as a businessman for some years in London, had become an apostle of reconciliation between Japanese and British veterans. He had been a quartermaster at Kohima. On reaching it, he told me, he found stores of rice in Naga Village which he recommended be moved to a safer location. Only a little was moved. Most was destroyed by British gunfire.

★ ★ ★

The battle of Kohima, which marked the westernmost limit of Japanese conquests in World War II, can claim to have been a turning point not only in the Burma Campaign, but in the tide of the whole war. If Sato had captured Dimapur, Subhas Chandra Bose's Indian National Army, which had units fighting alongside the Japanese, would have proclaimed the invasion of India as a war of liberation from British rule. Bose himself was reported to have been at Kigwema, a few miles from Kohima, during the battle. Bengal, Bose's home state, could well have risen in revolt and the Gandhi-led moderates in the Indian Congress Party would have been discredited. Air supplies from Assam to Kunming over 'The Hump' (the Himalayan range on the borders of north-east Burma and South China) for Chiang Kai-Shek's army – a key element in American plans to defeat Japan – would have been cut off. The British, ignominiously defeated by a numerically inferior Japanese force at Singapore, would have been confirmed as a spent power in Asia. The 2nd Division, the only major British formation east of Suez, long relegated to a military backwater, its capacity untested since its unplanned arrival in India, faced, suddenly, a supreme test on a battlefield not of its choosing and with a timetable which made a mockery of the shibboleths of military planning. Its defeat at Kohima would have been a *coup de grâce* to the disintegration of Britain's Asian empire.

That a British division largely unblooded and strategically side-lined should have been flung piecemeal into an intense battle against the hitherto invincible Japanese was an ironic stroke of destiny unrecognized at the time by the American command, absorbed in the Pacific war, and the Allied command in Britain, which was focused on the impending invasion of Europe.

The Japanese advance on Imphal and Kohima had one positive side-effect – it temporarily halted the multi-lateral bickering among South East Asia Command and India Command and the Americans and the Chinese and Whitehall, all of whom had different agendas for dealing with the Burma front.

Sato was not the only General to be fired as a result of the battle of Kohima. After the siege of Imphal was raised, Major General John L Grover was relieved of command of the 2nd Division and demoted to a non-combatant post in England. No official explanation was given for this decision, which was regarded as unjust by everyone under Grover's command. When Lord Louis Mountbatten, after giving one of his all-pals-together talks to the troops, asked if there were any questions, someone said: 'Yes, sir. Why was our General fired?' Mountbatten equivocated.

The 2nd Division was not popular with the Indian Army, a proud hierarchy which regarded an all-British division as an intruder into its theatre of operations. The coolness with which the Division was regarded can be observed in a note, attached to a 2nd Division account of the battle, from HQ 14th Army to 11th Army Group on

August 8, 1944: 'Attached is a copy of an unofficial account of the battle at Kohima. I understand the account was compiled by 2 Div based on local information. Unfortunately no lessons are deduced, but the narrative of events may be of interest to you.'

One theory about Grover's dismissal was that the 14th Army was dissatisfied with the time taken to capture Kohima and subsequently to clear the road to Imphal. Major General Geoffrey Scoones, Commander of the 4th Corps in Imphal, was said by some to be the initiator of Grover's dismissal, but the deed was done by Lieutenant General Monty Stopford, Commander of the 33rd Corps with the authority of General Bill Slim, Commander of the 14th Army.

Another theory was that there was criticism in the UK of the 2nd Division's casualties. Whatever the reason, Grover was a sacrificial lamb. Fifty-eight years after the battle I met Lt Colonel David Grover, his son. 'Did your father leave any private papers?' I asked him. 'No.' 'Did he discuss with you the circumstances of his demotion after Kohima?' 'Never. He always said his first consideration was loyalty to the army.'

Grover's removal was more of a blow to the 2nd Division's morale than those who removed him realized. Generals are regarded by troops as akin to deities, distant but omniscient, above criticism – except in defeat. But this was a victory. Backbiting in high quarters, concealed from the hoi polloi in wartime, is sometimes revealed in memoirs written long after the event. But Grover's love of and loyalty to the army kept him silent. The durable affection and respect in which John Grover was held by those under his command were illustrated to the author in a letter dated August 2004 from Rex King-Clark, who commanded the 2nd Manchesters, the Division's machine-gun regiment. At the age of ninety-one, King-Clark wrote:

'I started to write something here about John Grover's abrupt dismissal. But I began to feel bitter so I've cut it out! After all, for years he had trained and readied us for battle in a variety of widespread roles – and when the Battle came, his 2 Div won it. And then he was sacked.

'In a way J G was 2 Div. He was admired and respected at all levels – and had the welfare of the rank and file, particularly, very much at his heart. Perhaps not charismatic, but faithful and true to those he served. A fine soldier in every sense of the word was John Grover.'

General Slim himself almost had a similar experience in May 1945 when he was demoted by General Oliver Leese, newly arrived from command of the 8th Army in Europe and acting, some said, on the instructions of Mountbatten, who was believed to be jealous of Slim. But Slim fought back. No quiet acquiescence here. Leese was ousted and Slim retained his command of the 14th Army, which was and is, to this day, gloriously identified with his name.

General Grover was at the dockside in Southampton in October 1945 to welcome the Division's return. He had been belatedly awarded a CB, a high honour not usually given for active service, either as a token to palliate an injustice or in recognition of his subsequent service. The depth of the bond between him and his troops can be observed in his farewell message, dated July 5, 1944:

'I wish to thank all ranks from the bottom of my heart, for the unexampled loyalty and service they have given me during the long period of my command. No commander could have had a greater honour than to command such a splendid body of men, with such a magnificent Divisional spirit, and so imbued with the determination to fit themselves to meet and defeat the enemy when their turn should come. That turn has come, and I am indeed proud to know how worthwhile all that long and stern period of training has been, and how magnificently the Division has lived up to its great reputation and traditions.

'To you has fallen the signal honour of being the first British division to achieve a major victory against our Japanese enemies.

'I thank you for the magnificent response you have invariably given me, whether in training or in setting an example of soldierly bearing and discipline in all your doings, or in the extremely testing calls I have had to make anew during our recent operations. I am indeed grateful ...

'I wish you all the best of fortune and success in all your future operations. I am indeed proud to have had the honour of serving in and commanding the 2nd Division.'

★ ★ ★

After three weeks on 5120, the Camerons were withdrawn to an area near Jotsoma, on a hillside leading to Mount Pulebadze, on the slopes of which the Norfolks had made their bold and arduous right hook which helped to clinch the Kohima victory. Alongside us in this rest area was the 2nd Battalion of the Durham Light Infantry. Chatting with two young subalterns, I noticed how they addressed each other with elaborate and subdued courtesy. Then I realized that they were jointly in charge of the battalion, being the only officers left unscathed after the terrible battle on the Ridge.

Because of the inaccessibility of this 'rest' area, a medical officer from another unit alternated with Peter Barkey in taking sick parades. Peter's sick parades were better attended than his colleague's. Peter was a natural humanitarian, who listened carefully to each Jock who reported sick and chatted with him. His colleague was likely to say: 'Dose of the shits, eh? Here, take this. Next!' Peter was a gentle philosopher, not ashamed to weep when two of his stretcher-bearers were killed on 5120; conscious always of both the stupidity of war and of his role as a healer and comforter; ready always to talk reflectively with his brother officers.

Peter and Frankie Maclauchlan, our padre, could have reversed roles. Medical Officers and padres both get attentive audiences on battlefields. Frankie was as likely to be seen hefting a box of ammunition up a slippery slope as sitting quietly in the dark among Jocks newly returned with their dead and wounded and asking if they 'would mind' if he read a passage from the Bible. Frankie would pray over the battlefield graves of soldiers whose hands Peter had held as they died.

From Jotsoma, I led two long-distance overnight patrols. The Aradura Spur, behind Kohima, straddling the road to Imphal, was the next objective, manned by a Japanese rearguard under the command, I learned later, of the formidable Major Nishida, who had secretly reconnoitred the route of the Japanese advance and had recovered from his wounds at the battle of Sangshak. I met Nishida over dinner with a group of Japanese veterans in Tokyo in 1989. He looked a tough hombre and I was glad I had not got any closer to him than I did.

Five of us set out to reconnoitre the Aradura Spur, passing the famous features of the Ridge – the tennis court where the Dorsets had given their virtuoso performance, Garrison Hill which the Royal West Kents had defended against overwhelming odds, the DIS and FSD features, including the spot where Lance Corporal Harman had won his Victoria Cross, Jail Hill, and GPT Ridge which the Norfolks had stormed from the south and near which Captain Randle had won his VC. These battle sites were all west of the road. The Aradura Spur fell away to the east. The idea was that we might attack, just for once, from above. Our first patrol got lost in the dense darkness and we had to hold onto one another to make sure we did not get separated. Then we were almost wiped out by a cluster of mortar bombs from our own side, not, however, fired by the Camerons, whose mortar platoon under David Murray was at that time in reserve. David was one of the small band of Cameron officers who served solidly throughout the campaign. He had been deeply affected by what he considered to be the unnecessary death of his close friend Johnnie McNaught. Blunt-spoken, with a short fuse, a strong disciplinarian, David was to become a professional soldier after the war and ended up as the Lieutenant Colonel commanding the Territorial Battalion of the Regiment in Inverness. As a hobby, he was a fine piper and in his later years wrote the standard work on the music of the Scottish regiments.

Our second patrol, east of the road, was more productive. We were able to get onto the actual Spur, passing, discouragingly, the corpses of an Indian patrol. We rather hoped that the Japanese would fire on us (and miss!), so that we could locate them, beat a retreat and bring down artillery fire. But they were clever at letting small patrols pass unmolested in order to tempt larger targets. At dusk, we retired to the Ridge side of the valley facing the Spur and found a hole in the scrub which, we could tell by the detritus, had been occupied by a Japanese patrol. This gave us a good view of the Spur and, when light came, sure enough, wisps of smoke revealed that some careless Japanese had lit a fire and we were able to report where the Spur was occupied.

The divisional advance called for the 5th Brigade to cross the Ridge and descend to the valley at the foot of the Spur, and advance upwards (again!), the Dorsets leading the way. The first task allocated to the Camerons was to capture a small hill called The Pimple. It was assaulted successfully by C Company, commanded by Angus Douglas. After it was occupied, with casualties on both sides, Douglas took a bullet in the neck. He was carried past me on a stretcher, the death pallor on his face. I learned afterwards that he had asked for a drink. The sergeant accompanying him had only whisky in his flask. Angus took a gulp, smiled, and died. He was a great old toper ('old' being in his thirties). Subalterns used to take bets on how many half pints of beer he could consume without leaving the room. But he was no beer belly. Slim and wiry, he finished regularly among the leaders of cross-country runs. I had the impression that Angus McAlester had his old friend's death on his conscience, since Douglas had briefly commanded the battalion in England and would normally have been second-in-command of the battalion, not the leader of a company assault.

There remained Big Tree Hill, the upper part of the Spur abutting the road to Imphal. I was asked to lead a patrol to ascertain enemy strength there but was recalled in the gathering darkness. Next morning, D Company lined up to assault Big Tree Hill in a set-piece attack, with tremendous artillery support. The upper part of Big Tree being free of jungle, Mike West and his staff had a grandstand view from the Kohima side of the valley. I carried a satchel of phosphorus grenades to fling in front of me to make sure the gunners knew where we were. As we approached the ridge of the Spur, they switched to solid armour-piercing shot which plugged into the foxholes just above our heads.

The Japanese did not simply steal away from Kohima. They conducted a resolute and stubborn series of rearguard actions to deny the road to Imphal, and give the remnants of their battered troops, many of them ill and starving, time to make their way across the hills to the River Chindwin. They still had some surprises, as the Division was to find as we advanced down the road towards Imphal.

Footsteps 1
Excerpts from Sylvia May's Diary

Kohima, December 2002

As soon as we checked in, Pfelie [Naga host] whisked us off to the Cameron Memorial on 5120. A lovely spot with stunning views, where the Camerons had their toughest battle. We found all the names that Dad had told us about and took photographs. The memorial is indeed in the middle of peoples' back yards, but is well looked after. We laid our poppy wreath with the Cameron tartan sash and took photographs. Pfelie said that he thought the memorial should be moved one day for safety. Memorials to other battalions are in the cemetery on the ridge. For our part, we like the thought of it remaining where it is, in the midst of people's lives.

For the evening we had a treat in store. We were welcomed by the elders of the Kohima Village. We were given rice beer and rice cake and a warm stone to sit on.

As we sat in a square, one by one they stepped up and told their wartime stories. It was fantastic. Each one had a story to tell. They all spoke of their love for the 'Britishers'.

These are translated summaries of some of the stories:
- *Our forefathers thought much of the British. We liked them very much. When they visit us, we feel as if we are returning from darkness to light.*
- *We used to kill our fellow-tribesmen. When the British came to our land they stopped us from killing people.*
- *During the war, our properties and our wealth were destroyed. After the war the British people have helped us to rebuild our houses.*
- *I am glad to know that your father is still alive and I am happy and thankful that you will be narrating our stories to him.*
- *I worked for the British army, spotting Japanese hideouts. Together with two sergeants I located the Japanese headquarters about 10 kilometres from here.*
- *When the British retreated from Dimapur, only the District Commissioner, Mr Pawsey, remained at Kohima. Being harassed by the Japanese, we assembled one day and decided to go to Dimapur and ask*

for help. Three of us met Commissioner Pawsey coming up the road on his motorbike. He was very happy and told us to go back to our villages but to hide in the jungle because there would be shooting.

- *After the British Army came they supplied us with twelve-bore guns. We used these against the Japanese.*
- *I was taken for forced labour by Japanese soldiers, tried to escape but was recaptured.*
- *My brother won the Military Medal, which was the only recognition we had from the British Government.*
- *After the battle of Kohima the British government gave us pieces of 'wriggly tin' [corrugated iron] to reconstruct our houses.*

In response to their speeches, Rob read out some of Dad's notes.

The Catholic Cathedral is a very modern structure built on the hill above the Imphal Road. In the grounds there is a 2 Div memorial plaque. In the immaculately kept war cemetery we located many Cameron graves. Dad had given us a list of some of his friends who had been killed. We located all of them except Tommy Cook, whose body was apparently never found.

The Grant tank is awesome. It really is just where it was abandoned in the battle, all skew whiff on the hillside. Pfelie suggested we should provide a legend, which he would arrange to have engraved on the stone, since many people wonder how the tank came to be there. *

We also visited the Naga museum and tried to learn something of the local culture. There are sixteen tribes in Nagaland. Most of the population is Christian. The first minister – an American Baptist – arrived in Nagaland in 1846. Each tribe has its own language, wears different clothes from the others and lives in different styles of house. The people who are looking after us are the Angami.

We went to the shops. The marketplace would be alarming to a vegetarian, with pieces of animal on display, also plastic bags of tiny live frogs and bowls of live silkworms. Nagas seem to eat everything that grows or moves. Pfelie said we wouldn't see any birds in Kohima. They've all been eaten. The Nagas wear shawls, each tribe having its own design, which is also a kind of tribal flag. We were honoured to receive several shawls as gifts.

We were shown the stadium, where 15,000 to 20,000 people were to gather the next day for a reconciliation ceremony. Each tribal leader will stand and solemnly pledge to forgive one another. There will be a huge fire in which each leader will symbolically burn the list of his tribe's griev-ances. We realized that our visit coincided with a major event in Naga history, portending hope for the future.

Later, Pfelie took us to see his house. Then on to the home of the recently retired Head of Forestry, who, although we were unannounced, received us warmly with coffee and cakes. Again we sat around for a long talk, this time about tree planting.

---

*AUTHOR'S NOTE: After Sylvia and Rob returned to England, we located the tank Commander – Major Ezra Rhodes – who by 2003 was ninety-two years old. His daughter and son-in-law brought him from his home in Bristol to our home in Marlow, and we asked him to tell the story. Beyond the front lines and under Japanese fire, the tank had slithered to a halt. Rhodes and his crew put the machine gun on automatic fire and managed to get back to the British lines on foot. After he reported to the brigadier, it was pointed out to Rhodes that blood was streaming from the back of his head, which he had not noticed. The inscription now on the stone is in Rhodes's own words. He died shortly after we met him.

The Cameron memorial in 1944 (*left*), revisited by the author in 2004 (*right*)

We had dinner at the hotel with Pfelie, his wife Khriesi, niece and driver. This family have really been fantastic. We have seldom met such warm and gentle people. Charles Chasie, whom we were due to meet, is up to his ears in the reconciliation programme and has been unable to meet us. He phoned tonight to apologize, which he really didn't have to do.

We talked about the idea of the Kohima Educational Trust, to be set up by the 2 Div veterans after their last reunion. This would be greatly welcomed by the Nagas. They need more books, educational materials and even teachers. We also talked about student exchanges and scholarships.

At the Baptist church in Kohima Village, we met the pastor, whose son Rob is sponsoring to go to school. Then off for another whizzy walk round 5120 and another look at the Cameron memorial. The whitewash has been removed as they thought it looked tacky. They are talking about moving it to another site nearby where the posts and chain which once surrounded it could be re-erected.

Next day we spent the morning at the cemetery. I counted sixty-one Cameron gravestones. Yesterday in Kohima Village one of the elders told us of a soldier's body buried on 5120 which was moved to the cemetery years after the battle.

We were invited to a New Year festival in Khonoma, high up in the hills beyond Jotsoma. At a viewpoint with fantastic views, huge vats of food were cooked over open fires. Speeches were made and songs were sung. We were given a tremendous welcome.

Rob went to Merema and met an old boy who had been there during the battle. He had been given a muzzle-loading rifle and had managed to blow some of his fingers off in attempting to load it. After the war there were thousands of British and Japanese guns piled up and abandoned. For the next ten years, until the civil war with India made guns illegal, every Naga had his own weapon.

We went down to Zubza and climbed above it to achieve the best view we could get of the whole Kohima battlefield. The view of Pulebadze (7,500 feet) which we had climbed yesterday, was crystal clear. We also found a memorial stone on a ridge below Pulebadze erected in memory of the Japanese.

Before we left for the drive down to Dimapur we were taken to see a series of trenches on the east side of 5120, dug by the Japanese. Overgrown, of course, but still clearly visible.

In these ten days we have learned a great deal about the Naga people, their problems, their hopes and their fears. Our continuing memory will be the friendship and hospitality of the people.

Sylvia and Rob May with Naga villager at Khonoma, near Kohima, New Year's Day 2003

Chapter Six

Pursuit and Respite

... the race is not to the swift, nor the battle
to the strong ... time and chance happeneth
to them all. ECCLESIASTES 9:11

I SEEMED TO HAVE FORMED a reasonable rapport with Angus
McAlester, considering the differences in our ages and backgrounds. A product of Sandhurst, he did not discuss politics, women
or religion, subjects of absorbing interest to me. Like most regular
officers he was a serious, but quiet, drinker. He had his own vocabulary. He called the Japanese 'the Nip'. A motorcycle was a 'stink-
wheel'. My side of our infrequent conversations consisted mostly of
'Yes, sir.' If to vary it, I said, 'Very good, sir,' Angus would say
'You're not a bloody butler.' 'No, sir.' Like most regulars, he was an
admirer of physical prowess and enjoyed seeing me and my platoon
dangling over cliff sides or swimming for miles. He approved of my
marriage and was more amused than annoyed when my big explo-
sion landed a clod in our neighbouring battalion's soup.

I guess he felt I was reliable, although I had a tendency to exceed
my brief and make him nervous. I was called back a few times when
I was eager to push on. Colin Hunter, my Company Commander,
was a model of understanding, although on one occasion I heard
him remark wryly to Angus that D Company seemed to be more
often in the lead than the others.

Along with Angus Douglas, McAlester was the last Sandhurst
survivor in the Camerons. He had had a clubby relationship with
Skin Hickson and Peter Saunders but cannot have failed to observe
the low esteem in which these two were held both by those under
their command and those to whom they reported. Taking over
command in the battlefield, he knew very well that he depended
entirely on his officers, from whom, however, he felt culturally isolated. He was a vague soul, not a natural leader. He was the only
battalion commander in the 2nd Division to be awarded the DSO
and Bar in Burma.

In London in 1946, Angus asked me if I would sign on as a regular officer, which was a great compliment. I only saw him once after that, at the battalion's one and only reunion, held in Edinburgh in 1972. He was as vague and stiff as ever. In the 1990s I talked about Angus with a friend who had been on the faculty of the Royal Military College at Shrivenham, where Angus had been in charge of the married quarters for twenty years. Referring to Angus's decorations, he remarked that 'he must have had bloody good company commanders.'

Among the Cameron officers, an outstanding example of discipline, leadership and modesty was Bill ('Dave') Davidson. Born in Edinburgh in 1916 and already a practising solicitor when the war broke out, he commanded B Company throughout the campaign with quiet courage and judgment in achieving objectives with minimum casualties. Wounded on 5120, he refused to be evacuated. He was much in demand throughout his military service as a defending officer in courts martial and won most of his cases. Dave was one of the organizers of the battalion's reunion in 1972, by which time he was a Writer to the Signet, high up in the Scottish legal profession. His hobby was rhododendrons, which kept us in contact, because he consulted me about getting a book published on the subject. Dave was awarded a belated and much deserved MC. I last saw him when he and David Murray and I met over lunch at the Gordon Arms, an old inn in the Ettrick Valley of the Scottish Borders. He died in 1999.

When I read the proofs of this book in 2005, the only other surviving Cameron officers who had fought in the Burma Campaign were David Murray, Peter Grant and Allan Roy. Peter was the signals officer for most of the campaign. Like David Murray's mortars, the signals gave indispensable support to all four companies. Peter was a highlander from Drumnadrochit near Inverness, with a pawky, never-failing sense of humour. His book *A Highlander Goes to War* (Pentland Press 1995) is the only published account by a Cameron about the Burma Campaign, apart from Volume 5 of the Regimental Records, published in 1952. He died in August 2005.

My company runner, George Major, who became an insurance agent in Wales after the war, reminded me on a recent Christmas card of my efforts to get the Jocks to sing. They sang best about three o'clock in the morning, when they were cold, wet and miserable. It sounded more like keening than singing. It was regarded as a last resort to keep their spirits up. George told me that when he accompanied me to battalion headquarters he would eavesdrop so that he could tell the lads what was going on. Fortunately, I never concealed anything from them. The Jocks did their duty and kept quiet about it. They always expected the worst, and most of the time they were right.

The compatibility of the Yorkshire and Scottish temperaments was important to the solidarity of the battalion. All British units in the Burma Campaign had to be self-contained. This was not a war of liberation. We were met by no cheering crowds, no garlands, no kisses, no tears of joy. We were strangers in strange lands. The battalion was our world, and, along with the rest of the Division, we took perverse satisfaction in being part of 'The Forgotten Army'.

★ ★ ★

The advance beyond Kohima began on June 6, 1944, D-Day in Normandy. The first half of the eighty miles from Kohima to Imphal switchbacks across forest-clad valleys and steep ridges, ideal defence country. The steepness of the ridges, rising and falling on either side of the road, made it difficult to move round flanks. The three brigades of the 2nd Division took turns in leading, making right or left hooks, across rain-soaked valleys and up slippery paths to villages, all built defensively on the tops of hills in the Nagas' head-hunting days.

The Camerons' War Diary records engagements at Pfuchama, Phesama, Kigwema and Jakhama. Dossing for the night in a flea-ridden *basha* (hut) in one of these villages, I slept under a wall on which a Japanese had written in English: 'You have tanks and planes. We come back.' Most of the Japanese survivors from Kohima were to perish. The paucity of surviving Japanese witnesses of Kohima is revealed in the bibliography of books in Japanese about the campaign. There are seventy-two books about Imphal, only six about Kohima.

The Camerons' sharpest engagement on the road to Imphal was at Viswema. The leading company, under Jimmie Somerville, had four killed and fourteen wounded trying to get past a Japanese roadblock. It had been a mistake to try to break through at the level of the road, where the *khud* (bank) fell away steeply to the left, while to the right, indenting the equally steep hill, was a deep gully where the Japanese had dug in on both sides. Whichever bank you tried to climb, they shot at you from the other.

D Company was then ordered to make a right hook, unfortunately without reconnaissance. Making our way in single file in the dusk along the jungle-covered hillside above the road, we were either so silent or so lucky that we found ourselves in the midst of the Japanese positions, undetected by them. I broke the silence by shooting three Japanese who were unwarily moving outside of their foxholes. Then, as the saying goes, all hell broke loose. Lance Corporal Harrison, a burly professional rugby player, who was point man just ahead of me, was shot in the leg and asked permission to withdraw. The next time I saw him was at the battalion reunion in Edinburgh in 1972. He told me he had been able to resume his rugby career.

The Jocks filing immediately behind me had found they were standing on top of a foxhole, so they leaned over and slipped grenades into the firing aperture. By this time it was getting dark. We slithered down the hillside and formed a defensive box on a slight bump. Colin Hunter said to me: 'Do you think we can stay here?' I said no. Just then Japanese machine guns opened up, their lines of fire converging where we crouched. One of those killed was Sergeant McCassey, who was standing above me. He was not a natural soldier. He had to force himself into action. His face used to turn an alarming shade of grey before he set out on patrol. But he never shirked. He wrote home often, with photographs of his wife and children open on his knee. Why he was standing above me, smiling, when the crossfire caught him, I have no idea. He was a brave man because his fear was palpable.

In that moment we had three killed and six wounded. Stan Mawdsley, my batman, demonstrated his athleticism by running back to battalion headquarters with a bullet in his thigh. 'I felt it would stiffen up if I didn't keep moving, sir,' he explained. On such occasions, my language deteriorated into strings of expletives, which perhaps got more attention by being uttered by one who was usually pure of speech. But no amount of cursing could make that position tenable. As at Kohima, we were below the Japanese. Obviously this attempted right hook had become an infiltration. We withdrew with our dead and wounded.

The following night I was ordered to take a patrol – radio operator, Bren gunner and two riflemen – to a much higher altitude. We started at dusk in a gully half a mile behind our lines and emerged at first light above the tree line into scenery reminiscent of the Scottish highlands, hills covered with gorse, bracken and coarse grass. This time we not only got above the Japanese but behind them, and could see their neatly dug trenches on each pimple of the ridge below us. After descending back to the road, I was asked to report to Mike West, and noted that General Grover was also present.

The next night (starting at 3.30 am, according to the War Diary) I was able to lead D Company right onto the highest Japanese redoubt. Dave Davidson's B Company took over the lead and worked their way down the ridge to meet up with our brother battalion, the Worcesters, who had taken over the advance down the road. CSM Geordie Kerr, an avuncular and highly respected figure, said to me as they set off, 'We've been lucky so far.' I said I didn't believe in luck. The recipe was judgement plus intuition.

I was becoming greatly intrigued with the Japanese mentality. The three Japanese I shot at Viswema seemed to me not to have dived for cover as fast as I would have in their situation. Also near Viswema, half a dozen Japanese bayonet-charged an entire company of a neighbouring battalion. Was this foolhardiness, courage or fatalism? I was told by someone that he saw a Japanese laugh when one of his comrades was shot. Hysteria, battle fatigue or insouciance? I wrote some of my reflections in a school notebook and passed them to Angus, who received them without comment. The burden of my essay was that by understanding better how the Japanese think, we would be able to fight them more effectively. By our standards, they were careless of danger and displayed more blind discipline than judgement in their reflexes. They did not seem to share our reluctance to be dead heroes.

While British officers in Burma took care to dress indistinguish-
ably from their men, Japanese officers were recognizable by their
swords. Theirs was no citizens' army. The officers were mostly mil-
itaristic by nature and treated their men harshly.

Two things had been drummed into us about the Japanese
before we encountered them. One was that they would rather die
than surrender and the other that they treated prisoners cruelly.
The most common word associated with the Japanese in the minds
of the British troops was 'atrocities'. In my note to Angus was the
thought that their reputation for ruthlessness tended to obscure
their weaknesses on the battlefield. Fatalism, I suggested, was not
bravery. No British general would have informed his troops, as
General Mutaguchi informed his invasion force, that few of them
would survive.

Differing attitudes to death meant that neither side treated the
other with any thought of mercy. There was no respect for a gallant
enemy, no thought of honourable surrender. In North Africa, the
British troops sang *Lili Marlene* as sentimentally as did their
German enemies from whom they learned it, and General Erwin
Rommel was respected by the British as a brilliant commander who
obeyed the rules of war. We had no rulebook, which clarified the
mind, but it was a nervous way to live.

★ ★ ★

After Viswema, we had to deal with the last Japanese roadblock at
Maram, south of which the valley widened and the mountains and
jungles were too far from the road to offer defensive positions. High
above Maram, some huge standing stones on a hill afforded a
strong defensive redoubt. I did not know about these stones when I
set out with my platoon to try to pinpoint the Japanese positions.
Clambering upwards, as we always seemed to be, I came to a cliff-
face. Left or right? My intuition said right, which was just as well,
because the Japanese were manning their trenches on the left hand
side of the hill behind the standing stones. Corporal McWilliams,
who was awarded the Military Medal for his exploits on this occasion, and I were able to occupy an empty Japanese trench, facing
inwards. We could hear the Japanese talking. McWilliams, a natural-
born fighter, wanted to charge ahead. I restrained him. 'We need

covering fire,' I whispered. When Willie Keir arrived with his Bren gun, I put him in the unoccupied trench, and spread the rest of the lads out ready for assault. Meanwhile, a Japanese machine gunner had crawled behind a low wall, about ten yards away and shot Willie through one of his pouches which contained a phosphorus grenade. He seemed to explode. I tried to keep the Japanese quiet with a few grenades and moved back to rescue Willie. I was joined by Lance Corporal Thompson, who was immediately wounded. 'Come on, lad,' I said to Willie. 'We'll get you out of here.' Holding his hand, I could feel another burst of fire into his thigh. Our eyes met. 'It's no use, sir,' he said. 'I'm fucked, I'm finished.' So I left him, and he has been on my conscience ever since. We withdrew some way down the hill to do what the Japanese hated most – bring down artillery fire.

Only when we advanced again and found the Japanese gone did I see the standing stones under which they had been sheltering. Behind the low wall over which I had been lobbing grenades at the Japanese gunner, there was a pool of blood. Willie's body lay where I had left him, minus Bren gun. We dug a shallow grave, Frankie said a prayer and planted a simple cross to guide the exhumation team. Willie was a wee Glasgow welder and a romantic. His favourite song, which he sang lugubriously now and then, was:

I'm the last of the Texas rangers
And I ride the prairie all alone.
I'm the last of the Texas rangers.
M' buddies has all gone home.

★ ★ ★

The road to Imphal was now undefended. Our tanks rolled down it, firing at Japanese sighted on the foothills to the east. They were still desperately trying to shield their line of retreat. After the road was opened, the Camerons were ordered to occupy a range of hills east of the road about ten miles from Imphal. The footpath running along the ridge was being used by the Japanese as an escape route, being parallel to the road. As so often, we bumped into them without warning and had three fatalities and one man wounded, whom Bertie Harvey pulled to safety. Bertie, who was then adjutant, was a gymnast and athlete, but of diminutive stature. He once said to me, 'Gordon, I would give my soul to be six inches taller.' I pointed out to him after this exploit that being small had some advantages.

Our entry into Imphal was anti-climactic. The Japanese had never penetrated the Imphal Plain. The garrison had been supplied by air, and shielded by the 17th Indian Division on the Tiddim Road; the 23rd Indian Division on the road from Palel to Tamu; the 5th and 20th Indian Divisions on the northern fronts.

After we were established in Imphal, reinforcements arrived for us and the other depleted battalions. They were mainly anti-aircraft gunners who had been stationed in Ceylon, which was no longer under threat by Japanese air attack. Those who were drafted to the Camerons had all been in the same battery, so they were kept together in the re-formed A Company, which had been disbanded after Viswema. To my surprise and pleasure, it was placed under my command.

★ ★ ★

Our stay in Imphal was a pause for breath. The battalion had been in action for ten weeks. We felt we had learned what war was about. The politicians and generals say it's about victory; the soldiers know it's about survival.

On the battlefield, mourning is a private affair. It's almost as if those who were killed or the wounded who did not return were posted away. You close ranks, and there are promotions, replacements and reinforcements. The institution is impervious to casualties, up to a certain level. No units of the 2nd Division were in danger of disintegrating, although some were badly shaken. One Cameron Company had to be dispersed after Viswema. But hierarchic discipline can keep even a remnant going.

We were participating, although we did not know it, in the last low-tech war, fought by foot soldiers for territory. The jungle-covered hills on the Burma-India border and the limited supplies sent to the Burma front by both the Allied and Japanese high commands combined to provide an arena for small-scale battles and close combat. People back home thought that jungle warfare must be terrifying, but at least you didn't get wiped out en masse. In Burma we had more influence over our fate than sailors on warships and submarines or airmen in bombers and fighters, or, for that matter, men in rifle companies in Europe.

The opposing armies in Burma were roughly matched in numbers – about 300,000 on each side. The Japanese were the more cohesive, with only the Indian National Army as an ally. The 14th Army consisted of many nationalities both at the level of command and of manpower, the coordination of which was a challenge to Mountbatten and Slim. The altercations between them and Stilwell have been well documented, as have Stilwell's differences with Chiang Kai-Shek. Less has been said about, for example, the East and West Africans fighting in the 14th Army, some of whom feel to this day that their achievements have not been fully recognized. And almost nothing has been written about the tension between the 2nd Division who had felt orphaned till they won their spurs at Kohima, but who were considered arrogant, and the predominantly Indian-Army-derived 14th Army Command.

None of these perceptions was visible at company level in the Cameron Highlanders. We were too small, too segregated to have any strategic perception, and too preoccupied to engage in political or philosophical analysis. After all, the entire 2nd Division formed only 5% of the 14th Army and the Camerons formed only 5% of the 2nd Division. We were insignificant in the sweep of history.

Shortly after our arrival in Imphal, General Grover paid the battalion a farewell visit. This was followed by a hello visit by his successor, General Cameron Nicholson, who came to be much respected. Bill Slim also paid us a visit, making little impact, at least at company level – unlike Louis Mountbatten, whose folksy glamour suggested that he cared. Perhaps, like the 2nd Division, he was made to feel an uninvited guest in India. But he had the muscle and charm to sweep animosities aside. British wartime soldiers in India were unwitting inheritors of historic antipathy between the British and Indian armies, understandable between the representatives of an imperial power and those of a subject nation. But the Indian Army had acquired an aura of its own, separate from India as a nation, under the command of British officers who identified with the men they commanded. Both had their immediate loyalty first to the army they had built together and then to their respective nations.

My first contact with Indian troops in action was three weeks after we arrived in Imphal, when the 5th Brigade was moved onto the Shenam Ridge, on the road between Palel and Tamu. The Camerons took over from a Sikh battalion, commanded by an enormous and cheerful Lieutenant Colonel, his turban immaculate, his beard glistening in the monsoon rain in which they had been fighting for weeks. As he handed over his collection of water-filled trenches on a muddy hillside, I saw something in him that was new to me: relish for war. The Sikhs gave every impression of enjoying themselves. Volunteers to a man (like all the Indian regiments) they were professionals from a warrior race. The British regiments had few professional soldiers and had lost their strong regional identities after Dunkirk. Their performance in Burma drew as much on moral fibre as instilled discipline.

The night we took over from the Sikhs, a daring Japanese patrol had infiltrated onto the plain at Palel and planted explosive charges on British fighter planes parked there. My jovial Sikh friend seemed to regard this as a kind of escapade; an attitude not shared by the RAF flight crews whose defences had proved inadequate.

The battle for the Palel-Tamu road had been won by the 23rd Indian Division, of which the Sikh regiment was part, before we arrived. We advanced through the debris of battle, which included Japanese corpses tossed down the *khud*, which did not seem right to me. Dead soldiers should lie where they fall, or be moved respectfully after the battle is over, until they are buried.

We had only one casualty in the advance towards Tamu. For the first time since 5120 we were supplied by air, and had not become accustomed to its dangers. As I was talking to one of the new arrivals from Ceylon, Sergeant Major Toon, he was hit by a free-falling box of ammunition and killed instantly. Another needless death. Another graveside service by Frankie. When we got onto the plains of Burma, airdrops were better organized, with clearly marked target areas free of troops. When a drop was finished, a company of infantry would move over the dropping area and assemble the supplies in a central dump, always a popular assignment with the Jocks, whose battledress pockets bulged suspiciously when the job was done.

On our march to Tamu about 100 Camerons fell out with heat-stroke. Tamu itself was an utterly new experience, because we actually met some Japanese. The town was devastated and deserted except for corpses of civilians and Japanese soldiers, as it had been two years earlier following the terrible retreat from Burma, but then the corpses were British and Indian. My company was ordered to make a sweep through several villages to the east. At the first of these, I asked the headman if there were any Japanese there. He nodded, but first handed over two Indians from the Indian National Army, and gave me a message from a Lieutenant Brown, who, with five British soldiers, had passed through the village a few days earlier as prisoners of the Japanese.

Then the headman took me to a *basha* where I met my first Japanese. He lay helpless, clad only in a loincloth. There were pools of urine in the hollows of his groin. I looked in his face and he in mine. His gaze was mild, passive. This was not what war was supposed to be about. 'Get a stretcher,' I said. Soon four Jocks were striding across the paddy fields carrying their emaciated enemy. Expecting to be ruthless, they suddenly rediscovered that it takes two to make a quarrel. We took twenty-eight prisoners on that strange day. Many were sick and starving, and some were young and frightened. Why, I wondered, had they been abandoned? No food, no medicine. Some of them were remnants of the force which had besieged Kohima.

Returning to Tamu, we encountered an advance unit of the 11th East African Division, who were about to undertake an arduous campaign in the monsoon in the Kabaw Valley, in the direction of Kalewa, the crossing point over the Chindwin into the plains of Burma. What strange war had brought black men to assist white men to fight yellow men in a country to which none of them belonged? The Africans were very tall and did not speak English. One of them picked up one of my diminutive prisoners and started cuffing him round the head, knocking his spectacles off. 'Put him down,' I said. Staring at one another, the three of us formed a momentary tableau. Slowly the African released the young Japanese.

I wish I could say that the Jocks were moved to humanitarianism by the experience of that day. A burst of Sten gun fire followed by screams from where an outlying platoon was picking its way among jungle hovels was claimed by 'Teeps' Laidlaw, a grizzled long-service sergeant, to be a response to a Japanese reaching for a grenade. I didn't believe him.

By the roadside, we came on a Japanese officer lying against a tree. Squatting by his side, brushing flies from his face, watching his every move, was his batman. Both were dressed in immaculate white. The officer spoke good English. He had been a businessman in Shanghai. Too weak to converse, he merely requested that he be segregated from the other prisoners.

We delivered our prisoners to a field ambulance unit at Battalion HQ. One of the Jocks started knocking a prisoner about. A Royal Army Medical Corps lieutenant colonel said sharply: 'Stop that! We have to live with these people after the war.' That was a new thought.

The next time we were to pass through Tamu, on the advance to the Irrawaddy, we were back in business and so were the Japanese. The interlude of humanity was forgotten. But first we moved back to Imphal on the trucks which had brought the Africans, and then back towards Kohima as far as the 82nd milestone, near the village of Maram, where we were to encamp, recuperate and retrain.

★ ★ ★

Everyone was given leave to destinations of their choice in India, some electing for the city lights of Bombay and Calcutta, others heading for the Himalayan foothills around Darjeeling or Srinagar in Kashmir. I was appointed Education Officer and sent on a week's course given by the Army Educational Corps at Pachmari, a hill station in central India, where Peggy joined me. After the course, we set off for Coonoor, in the Nilgiri Hills in South India, where the Milne family had rented a bungalow. It was October 1944 and Peggy was seven months pregnant, as was her sister Kitty, who had married Peter Pinfield, a naval officer.

I returned to Milestone 82 after three weeks, laden with books and gramophone records. We started a wall newspaper called *The Clachan Courier*, organized debates and concerts, arranged lectures on 'current affairs', and held a choir competition to Angus's irritation when he found earnest choristers rehearsing in corners of the camp. I invited three officers from the Royal Welch Fusiliers to be judges on the grounds that the Welsh knew how to sing. The winning entry was *Abide With Me*.

The camp was on lush grass-covered hillsides which we found, to our cost, harboured ticks which caused typhus. We had thirteen cases, all of whom died. Drums of DDT were rushed in and we soaked our clothes in the stuff. Banned twenty years after the war because it damaged the environment, this chemical was a lifesaver then. Like many inventions, it was discredited by its misuse.

Our time at Milestone 82 included a pilgrimage to Naga Village to set up the Camerons' war memorial, a bronze plaque on a rugged stone, designed by Alan McKillop, one of our officers, with the words 'Lochaber No More' inscribed below the ninety-six names. Lochaber is the Cameron country in the Scottish Highlands. *Lochaber No More*, a pipe tune, is a lament for soldiers who march away, never to return.

On October 18, 1944 a Cameron contingent joined those of other 2 Div regiments, to inaugurate the Division's Memorial at the crossroads in Kohima, with its inspired and oft-quoted inscription:

> When you go home
> tell them of us, and say
> for your tomorrow
> we gave our today.

★   ★   ★

Exalted thoughts were rare at Milestone 82 in 1944. For relaxation, we had one or two movies and concert parties. We also arranged rugby matches on the polo ground in Imphal, and one or two of us volunteered to assist air supply drops over the Kabaw Valley. You tied yourself with a rope to a stanchion on the closed side of the circling plane and lent out of the open door on the other side, pushing loads out as close as possible to the appointed site.

Of course, there were parades and inspections and training, especially for reinforcements, who included an intake of newly-commissioned second lieutenants, who, to my twenty-four-year-old eyes, were young. Asked to conduct a battle course for them, I did not have to go far for practical case studies. We climbed, and re-climbed, the hill above Maram, letting the battle unfold and posing at key points the question: 'What would you have done?' Many who had sailed on the *Marnix* in April 1942 had now been killed, wounded or posted elsewhere. Leadership at the platoon level for the next stage of the campaign was to fall on young men who were new to foot-soldiering. I was fortunate to have Mike Spreckley, John Waring and Gordon Duff as my platoon commanders.

Footsteps 2

Excerpts from Sylvia May's Diary

MARAM, December 2002

As we approached Maram (which lies about half-way between Kohima and Imphal) the guides were planning the stop we had requested. What we didn't expect was to be welcomed by the Fathers of the Don Bosco School, built, along with a church, on what may well have been the site of the Maram battle in 1944. Father Joseph told us they had found all sorts of military detritus whilst laying the foundations. They are now building a sports ground and human resource centre. They have over 1,600 pupils at the school and have just opened a college.

Pulling up unannounced, we were immediately invited for coffee and breakfast. I was hungry. We had been on the road for three hours, so this seemed a perfectly wonderful invitation.

Father Joseph took us on a tour of the school, throwing in nuggets of information about the battlefield which we eagerly absorbed. Dad had talked about a stone wall over which he had thrown grenades and standing stones behind which the Japanese had sheltered. We found them both.

Father Joseph still had things to show us. He wanted us to meet The Queen. She lives in the oldest house in the village and is an 'ancient-in-appearance' woman. Father Joseph called to her but she was reluctant to show herself. We never did find out why she is The Queen. Father Joseph then suggested we joined the school for open lunch, which means simply eating outside from a large trestle table laden with huge bowls of rice and curry. Before lunch we had met Father Paolo, who is clearly the Father of Fathers – a grand old Italian gentleman of ample girth and matching hospitality. We marvelled at the Italian-ness of one who had lived in India for sixty years and noticed the continual stream of pupils going to him for advice.

IMPHAL December 2002

Imphal is fabulous. The British and Indian war cemeteries are havens of well-tended repose. According to the visitors' book, someone from the 2nd Division has been here not long ago. We found the gravestones of four Camerons – Private Watson, who died in November 1944 and Lance Corporal Corrigan, Private Smith and Private Warren, who all died in June 1944. We were taken to still another war cemetery high on a hill. The whole plain of Imphal lay below us. The plaque was dedicated to the 'Stars of Manipur who laid down their lives for their motherland.' Looking north, I could see the road to Kohima; another road running eastwards must be the way to Tamu.

The people in Manipur are different from all the states we have visited in India, except Darjeeling and Sikkim. They don't hassle us. Most stare a lot. A few ask for their photos to be taken. Everyone is polite and gentle.

Up early and at the house of our host Yambem Laba by 8.30 am and off on the road to Tiddim. We had wanted to go to Palel, but learned that it was 'not possible today'.

We stopped at the Assam Rifles' barracks to see a Japanese tank, but they wouldn't let us in. Next stop the Manipur Rifles . They welcomed us warmly and allowed us to see their British tank. They even allowed us to take photographs provided we did not get their barracks on film.

Then on to the India Peace Memorial built by the Japanese. It says:

> *This monument shall stand as a prayer for peace and a symbol of friend-ship between the peoples of Japan and India in memory of all those who lost their lives in India during the last World War.*

An odd concept, I thought. Wasn't it the Japanese who started all this? We drove through lots of villages. The colour is fantastic. The girls wear brilliant reds, oranges and yellows – really bright. We stopped in one place to buy fruit and a stone pot. The landscape on either side of the Tiddim Road is either lakes or paddy fields. We travelled about twenty miles to Moirang, and stopped at a place marking a red-letter day – April 14, 1944 – 'in the history of the India's Freedom Movement'. The plaque reads:

> *On this occasion Forward Block pays its revolutionary tribute to the patriot of patriots, Netaji Subhas Chandra Bose.*

We tried to get into the Indian National Army War Museum, where the Netaji Library is housed, but it was a holiday.

Chapter Seven

Rivers to cross

'Let us cross the river and rest under the trees.'
Last words of STONEWALL JACKSON

BY DECEMBER 1944, we were on our way again, retracing our steps via Imphal, Palel and Tamu, to the Kabaw Valley, which had been cleared of Japanese in unpleasant monsoon fighting by the East Africans. Drearily, our first assignment was road repair, at Yazagyo north of Kalewa, where a pontoon bridge had been laid across the Chindwin. For three years, following the demoralizing British evacuation of Burma in 1942, the Chindwin had been the dividing line between Japanese-occupied Burma and India. Across it in their fabled, but strategically questionable 1943 adventure, the Chindits had paddled themselves into enemy territory. Across it, in March 1944 General Mutaguchi's three divisions had surreptitiously launched their bold and ill-fated invasion. Their starving remnants had struggled across it again in the months after their defeat. Now, on the longest floating bridge constructed in World War II, the 14th Army was crossing it once more – this time as pursuers.

Christmas came early for us in 1944. Turkey and plum pudding were airdropped near Kalewa on December 18. In the Kabaw Valley we had travelled in five-ton trucks whose Indian drivers had an alarming habit of falling asleep. At one point I took over the wheel, which the Jocks in the back found hilarious. (Was it my fault that the handbrake wasn't working?) After crossing the bridge, we advanced on foot, marching by night with the pipers playing to keep us awake.

Much of the route eastwards from Kalewa is through jungle, leading to the central plains of Burma, traversing territory the Japanese had decided not to defend. Marching single file along dry riverbeds of soft white sand, with the moon shining through the trees, we had time to observe that the country was beautiful. Gus Claxton, the padre of the Dorsets, liked to tell how he asked Peter Barkey, whom he found brooding at his field ambulance station,

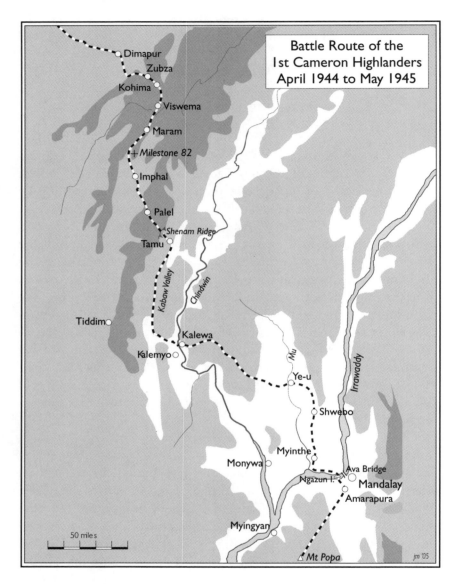

Battle Route of the
1st Cameron Highlanders
April 1944 to May 1945

'What are you thinking about?' Peter replied: 'I was just thinking how beautiful it is.' Peter was unusual in his capacity for philosophic detachment.

We reconnected with the Japanese some fifty miles from Kalewa after crossing the Mu River, which we forded silently at chest

82

height at 3 am on the day before Christmas. Whispering among ourselves as we dug in on the edge of a palm-fringed field, the moonlit silence broken only by the sound of temple bells, we could almost dream that we were on a night exercise. Any dreamlike thoughts were abruptly banished when one of our patrols met a bullock cart, laden with Japanese. Both sides were surprised. After confused fighting in a field of sugar cane, the patrol completed its sweep and I sent out another one, which stumbled over a prone Japanese who, after shooting one of our men dead, ran weavingly for cover under a hail of fire. Then silence. I lay next to a sharp-eared nineteen-year-old Highlander, far from his native Inverness. 'I can hear the teffils' he whispered to me, and sure enough there was the distinct sound of a body sliding towards us through the grass. John Waring threw a grenade, and there was silence again. At first light, we found the body of a Japanese officer who seemed to have been making a one-man suicide attack. The grenade had blown off his hand, which was still clasping his sword. In his satchel, we found papers which we sent back to Intelligence, and were congratulated because they set out the Japanese strategy for the defence of Shwebo, the main town between the Mu River and the Irrawaddy. Mac Ross, a tea planter from Ceylon who had been with the 2nd Camerons in North Africa and was at that time second in command of the company, led a third patrol which dispatched the remaining Japanese with the bayonet.

Played out in what felt like slow motion in the dawn light, these events again illustrated the unpredictable behaviour of the Japanese. In defence they were resolute and resourceful; in attack they were foolhardy and vulnerable. Now making a planned retreat to the east bank of the Irrawaddy which they hoped to hold, they would open fire from each tree-girt village. We would go to ground, call down artillery fire and, widely dispersed across the paddy fields, advance cautiously hoping that the Japanese had withdrawn. Sometimes we found only dazed villagers and wounded cattle. Those Japanese who had remained would take pot-shots at us before legging it to the next village.

Here on the plains of Burma, the Japanese had something they had lacked at Kohima: artillery. And they used it. One night when we were dug in near a crossroads, I found the trench I shared with Stan Mawdesley a little cramped and yielded it to him. In the early morning, the ever-polite Stan put an arm out of the trench to shake me awake: 'Excuse me, sir. We're being shelled.' Obviously, I had no trouble sleeping.

In the plains of Burma, the rifle came back into its own. Both sides could take cover and take aim. In one village, a Jock put his head through a hedge and a Japanese shot him through the face. His comrades carried him back on an old door torn from its hinges. One of the Jocks pointed out that there was a nail sticking into the man's leg. Somebody said: 'He's dead.' But it didn't seem right. I moved the dead man's leg to a comfortable position, free of nails. How details stay in one's memory.

Respect for the dead was as instinctive as succour for the wounded. A patrol sent to reconnoitre beyond a captured village returned after thirty minutes minus one man, who lay wounded somewhere in no man's land. By this time, we were fortunate to have a Burmese speaker from the Intelligence Corps attached to the battalion. Putting a grenade in each trouser pocket, I asked him if he would care to join me. Gallantly, he did, as did Corporal Shannon, one of my street fighters who loved to carry his Bren gun on a shoulder strap. Accompanied by two stretcher-bearers with morphine, we found Joe Lyons moaning softly in the twilight. Shannon could not be restrained from spraying every moving bush along the way. Back at the field dressing station, Peter Barkey tended Joe, who had been shot through the chest. When I asked Peter how he was, he held a finger to his lips, whereupon I launched into some cheerful chatter, which was the last thing Joe heard before he died.

★ ★ ★

On January 10, after we occupied Shwebo, a divisional signaller called me on the field telephone with a personal message. Peggy had had a stillborn child. I was readily granted compassionate leave, handed over command of the company and was on my way within an hour. A returning supply plane took me to Comilla, headquarters of the 14th army. There I told my story to a sympathetic transport officer who flagged down a US Air Force bomber which was already on the runway. The none-too-pleased crew opened the door and reached down for my up-stretched hands. I was at Calcutta's Dum Dum airport on the evening of the day I left. Next I had to talk my way onto the regular overnight military flight to Madras. Next morning, I was on the train to Coimbatore, which took me to the railhead of the Nilgiri Hills mountain railway at Mettapalayam and was at Peggy's bedside, 2,000 miles from Shwebo, forty-eight hours after getting the message, a gaunt and, I fear, grim figure.

The stillborn child had been a son. Peggy's sister, Kitty, had had her baby successfully a few days earlier. The doctor had no explanation. I stayed with her for three days and learned much about grace under adversity.

The journey back to Burma was not so fast. I had to travel by train from Calcutta to Dimapur and by truck once more the long road through Kohima, Maram, Imphal, Palel, Tamu, Kalewa to Shwebo. When I rejoined the battalion, after ten days away, not much had happened. We were halfway between Shwebo and the Irrawaddy, to the far bank of which the Japanese had now retired. I reflected that Joe Lyons had died at Peter's First Aid post on the same day that our son was stillborn.

★ ★ ★

On 8 February 1945, D Company was moved to the bank of the Irrawaddy in preparation for the divisional assault across the mile-wide river. We were stationed first in Myittha and then in Myinthe, neighbouring riverside villages demarcated by clumps of trees. Across the river lay the island of Ngazun, which peters into a sand bank downstream.

On the night before we moved to Myinthe, a Japanese landing party had surprised a company of Worcesters in Dawete, the next village downstream, three miles away. This raid turned into a disaster when the Worcesters mounted a counter-attack in which their battalion commander, adjutant and a company commander were all killed. The Japanese raiders then withdrew to the far bank, from which their gunners signalled their knowledge of our presence in Myinthe with occasional shells, causing us and the villagers to dive into foxholes, but otherwise life was quite peaceful.

Our supply trucks driving across the paddy fields raised clouds of dust, which no doubt helped the Japanese to range their guns. Peter Barkey visited us during one barrage and shared my foxhole, a rather superior structure with logs across the top, in the shelter of which we sipped coffee and ruminated, tensing up now and then for the next incoming shell. D Company headquarters was famous for its coffee, sent to me by Peggy in weekly packages, complete with sugar and condensed milk. To maximize the flavour, we never washed the coffee pot.

In fact, D Company lived rather well in Myinthe. Our Company Quartermaster was a good scrounger; the local sweetcorn was ripe. We purchased a pig which Sergeant Pickersgill, a butcher by trade, skillfully slaughtered, hung and bled from the branch of a tree before an admiring audience. The village headman lent me a table and a chair at which I wrote letters and my (subsequently lost) diary. The weather was perfect.

A few days after we occupied Myinthe, I was ordered to lead a night patrol to reconnoitre a landing site on the south bank. Neil White, who was by then commanding the Headquarters Company, came along, together with half a dozen officers and NCOs. We practised silent paddling in a backwater. Hoping that the Japanese would not be alert behind Ngazun Island, we steered round the sand spit and upstream in the channel between the island and the far bank. Above the narrow shore rose a twenty-foot high bank, topped with thick elephant grass up to eight feet high. We explored it thoroughly. It seemed to me that the elephant grass would be an asset, once the battalion got ashore. I was wrong. No battle goes according to plan.

We dispersed to search the grass and reassembled where we had disembarked, Neil and I sentimentally signalling to each other by whistling *The March of the Cameron Men*. We slipped back into the boat and let it drift downstream, easing it across the river, landing at Dawete just before dawn, giving momentary heart attack to a company of Dorsets who had taken over from the Worcesters and had not been informed about our expedition.

We abandoned our boat and walked the three miles to Myinthe. *En route,* in a fold of the open moorland, we found a dead British soldier, spreadeagled, face downward, rifle in hand pointing in the direction of Dawete. It was a mystery how the burial parties had missed him. He must have died alone. His tags identified him as Gunner Espey, one of the anti-aircraft gunners recently posted from Ceylon. On the previous day I had read a letter from him to the editor of the SEAC newspaper. Today he was a lonely, over-looked casualty of a battle too disastrous to be reported.

Visiting Myinthe fifty-seven years after the battle, Sylvia and Rob were shown seven unmarked graves in a field near the village. A farmer had discovered them while ploughing. A mystery. Who were they? One thing is certain: they had not been buried by their com-rades. If they had, the location of the graves and their identities would have been reported. Had they been in a firefight with the Japanese? Had they been prisoners? This corner of a foreign field will keep its secret.

The landing site we had scouted had also been recommended by an athletic Air Force Flight Lieutenant, a member of the Swimming Reconnaissance Unit, who operated alone on a paddle board. He told me that he had crossed the river the same night that we had to keep an eye on us. With his flippers he could move swiftly and almost invisibly on the surface of the water. It occurred to me, as we were planning this crossing, that our time spent at Juhu Beach preparing to land on the Arakan coast might not have been entirely wasted.

The following day I was given an aerial view of the prospective battlefield from a spotter plane. The pilot had the alarming ability, when I asked for a closer look at some feature, to fly the plane on its side so that I could look straight down. This made me airsick, but I did manage to notice that the elephant grass extended further than I had guessed – about a mile along the bank and a few hundred yards inland. Lacking manpower to defend the entire shoreline, the Japan-ese probably regarded the elephant grass as a good natural defence.

In some ways, an assault across a river is easier than a sea-borne landing. There are no waves. On the other hand, the current can be deceptive. Our D-Day was set for the night of February 24, with D Company as the leading wave. There were two differences between that night and the night of our reconnaissance. One was that the river was higher and the current stronger; and the other was that it was moonlight – factors which our high command had apparently either not noticed or decided to ignore. Probably there was a reason for haste, because three other divisions – the 19th (on our left, upstream) to the north of Mandalay, the 20th (on our right, downstream) and the 17th (further south, heading for Meiktila) – were already across the river. The 2nd Division was to link up with the 20th and advance on Mandalay from the west.

On the morning of the 24th I assembled my company of ninety-six men, after cutting eight small pieces of wood to represent our boats and laying them out on a primitive relief map, marked with twigs, on the ground. We would embark at 10 pm and go downstream in line astern until the last boat had passed the tip of the sandbank, and then turn in line abreast and head for the shore. Only ammunition, firearms and rations for forty-eight hours would be carried. Total silence would be observed. The men at the back of each boat had the pull cords of the outboard motors in their hands with orders to start the engines if the Japanese should open fire. We would land at the exact spot which we had reconnoitred, which meant going slightly upstream after rounding the sandbank. I went over it again and again. At the end, I read the 91st Psalm from my pocket Bible: 'Thou shalt not be afraid for the terror by night; nor for the arrow that flieth by day.' The Jocks listened intently and dispersed in silence. They never grumbled about going into battle, only about things like shortage of beer and cigarettes or non-arrival of mail. Bonded by being fed-up and far from home, all they asked was fairness under officers who shared their hardships, who told them everything they knew, who led the way and at least looked confident and cheerful. Given these conditions the Jocks displayed a dour aggressiveness and were fine soldiers.

After resting all afternoon, we had a big supper, downed the traditional tots of rum and queued silently for the boats. C Company, under Ian Swanson, along with Angus and battalion headquarters staff, was to tag on to our convoy after we passed their assembly point at Myittha, and then to perform the same manoeuvre that we were planning – turn to line abreast and land downstream of us. The river being faster than it had been on the night of our reconnaissance, rounding the spit into the current was harder. Just as we turned, Japanese machine gunners opened up. Bullets which did not find their mark made long whining noises as they skimmed off the water. 'Christ,' said Sergeant Major Mackie, crouching beside me. 'The bastards, the bastards!' screamed a wounded man from a nearby boat.

D Company got ashore with three killed and two wounded – low casualties because we were on the left and the machine guns were on the right, but also because of our readiness with the outboard motors. C Company caught the brunt of the firing. All in one of their boats were lost, except for Private Grimshaw who, his leg shattered by a bullet, floated five miles down the river and was picked up by 20th Division twenty-four hours later. Some of C Company's boats turned back, with their wounded. Peter Barkey got a bullet through the heart and died without a word. Frankie MacLauchlan had a bullet pass through the rim of his steel helmet, which can be seen to this day in the Regimental Museum in Inverness. A gunner officer accompanying Headquarters Company was wounded, leaving control of artillery support in the hands of his bombardier, who was to perform brilliantly.

On the shore, sheltered from the Japanese enfilade, D Company scrambled up the twenty-foot bank and charged through the elephant grass, colliding with stray Japanese who scurried away. Advancing as far as we could without losing touch with one another, we started to dig in on a perimeter stretching from the shore on our left to the left flank of C Company, about two thirds of whom had landed, on our right. I found Angus on top of the bank and informed him of this. Neil was on the shore below the bank, organizing the removal of the dead and wounded from the beached boats. He remained in charge of the beachhead for the next forty-eight hours and was awarded the MC for his 'magnificent leadership and utter disregard of danger'. Sergeant McEvoy, Peter Barkey's deputy, was awarded the Distinguished Conduct Medal for his care of the wounded.

We had established a tiny bridgehead, but couldn't make it secure until we had located and extirpated the Japanese machine gunners, hidden in the elephant grass which, I had believed, would be our ally. Patrols from C Company could not find them due to the density of the grass. Subsequently I formed the theory that the Japanese withdrew from their positions when we had no boats on the water. In our bridgehead, we were protected because they couldn't see us.

We were now in a dilemma. We couldn't extend our perimeter to the edge of the elephant grass without more manpower, yet our incoming reinforcements had to run the gauntlet of the Japanese guns. We did not know that the Worcesters, downstream from us, had been shot out of the water and had had to return to the north bank with some of their boats leaking. The Royal Welch Fusiliers, however, had taken Ngazun Island with some casualties. We were alone on the south bank.

B Company under Dave Davidson was the next to embark from Myinthe. There was a shortage of assault boats, so six amphibious landing craft (DUKWs), intended to carry supplies, were loaded with troops. Surprise now being lost, all craft used their motors from the outset. One of the DUKWs got across with some casualties, but two others were stuck on the sandbank, where they came under fire. By now it was daylight, and the Japanese were shelling the embarkation point, mortaring the stranded DUKWs and firing at any craft approaching the bridgehead. Nonetheless, most of B Company got across and took up a position between C and D Companies, enabling the perimeter to be extended.

Now that it had been proved practical to round the sandbank and land out of sight of the Japanese machine gunners, it seemed safe to embark A Company in the same small boats that we had used. The motor of one of these broke down and it drifted below the Jap guns. We watched in horror as the entire headquarters of A Company, including the Company Commander Johnnie Bain, were picked off one at a time. Some jumped overboard and attempted to swim ashore, crying for help, till they sank one by one, leaving only bloody bubbles. One of the drowning men with his last gesture pointed to where the Japanese guns were located.

Angus sent Peter Grant, who was now adjutant, back to Myinthe, where brigade headquarters was established and under shellfire. We needed air and artillery support, which was quickly forthcoming.

On the afternoon of the 25th, the Japanese positions were blanketed with artillery fire, and dive-bombed by a Hurri-bomber.

By the evening of the 25th, all four Cameron companies had crossed. D Company was then switched to the right flank and allocated a section of machine guns from the Manchester Regiment and an FOO from the 10th Field Regiment of the artillery. During the night of the 25th and 26th we managed to drive the Japanese out of the grass – a sort of pheasant shoot – to the west. Now they had nowhere to hide. We dug in about fifty yards from them. They were in a sugarcane field. We could hear them talking. We could bring down our guns exactly on their positions.

Reinforcements were now able to pour into the bridgehead. The Worcesters landed and captured Ngazun village. A disaster was averted when a pontoon raft loaded with men of the Royal Berks and Norfolks, swinging wildly behind its towing motor boat, began to career past us towards the Japanese positions. This time we could see what we were doing and were able to bring down machine-gun fire, smoke and artillery, while the pontoon raft managed to touch down on the outer fringe of the territory we held, and all on it were disembarked safely.

For a time D Company was very exposed, with enemy on three sides. But by the evening of the 26th, our tanks had landed at our bridgehead, led by a bulldozer which carved a road up the bank. Early in the morning of the 27th, one of our patrols found the Japanese gone, leaving foxholes and provisions indicating a force of about seventy men.

The Division now had a sizeable bridgehead. I handed our position over to a company of Norfolks, whose commander was embarrassingly complimentary about our well-dug foxholes and well-placed barbed wire. 'We like tidy battlefields,' I said modestly. Summoned into reserve, we were astonished to see tanks charging down a track carved from the point where we had landed only 48 hours earlier.

Slightly to our embarrassment, General Nicholson saluted us as we marched by. A few days later, he wrote a personal letter to Angus in which he said that the divisional crossing would have failed had it not been for the Camerons. The cost to the Camerons had been eighteen killed, twenty-five wounded and eight missing.

Footsteps 3

Excerpts from Sylvia May's Diary

KALEWA, *December 2002*

As usual we had got up at 5 am for our drive to Monywa where we would stay the night and buy tickets for tomorrow's boat up the Chindwin to Kalewa. Now we are off the tourist route. The hotel is a series of wooden chalets linked by a verandah. We wanted to stroll the streets, but were given a tour of more Buddhas. Our guard ... I mean guide ... didn't want to lose sight of us, so we walked around together. Rob spotted a barbershop and decided to have his hair cut, which was a laugh. We bought food for the trip to Kalewa. We are looking forward to twenty-two hours on the boat with nothing to do but read or sleep.

You can see too many sunrises, but I wouldn't want to have missed today's, as we sail up the Chindwin on Christmas Eve. Very romantic. We have our own cabin and are almost the only passengers. No other Westerners. The boat keeps getting stuck on sandbanks. They have a guy up front with a long pole who gauges the water's depth, and shouts to the captain, who tells the pilot which way to go. Very hi-tech. Locals catch the boat by getting alongside it in a skiff and jumping.

We sat up on deck pretty much all day, reading and playing chess. In the evening, we were shown the cockpit, expecting to see nothing more than a steering wheel. But they have a radar screen which no one apparently has been taught to use. There are about seven members of the crew in the cockpit, all shouting. Rob put up a mosquito net for me which was great, and we were again very pleased with our sleeping bags and grateful to have our Angami blankets.

We were roused by villagers crowding round the boat selling bananas, green vegetables, cooked chicken and giant freshwater prawns. This is obviously the regular breakfast stop. We are careful what we eat. Our guide has made sure the boat had purified water for us to cook our pot noodles.

The boat docked at Kalewa at 4.40 pm, having been due at 6 am. But we're not in a rush. Walking down the gangplank was a great balancing *act. Our guide expected a car to meet us, but it wasn't there, so we got on the bus to Kalemyo. Excellent fun! The bus had to keep stopping because of us. Each time we paid more. People jumped on and off, some carrying chickens. The road we followed leads to Tamu (access to which had been denied) and when we forked left for Kalemyo, we could only stare wistfully to the north where we really wanted to be heading. The Camerons marched down this road just before Christmas 1944 on their way to cross the Chindwin and on to Ye-u. From where the boat had docked we saw the road to Ye-u disappear tantalizingly into the trees on the other side of the river. This was the place where the 14th Army built the longest ever Bailey bridge to carry men and transport into the plains of Burma.*

It was dark by this time and we drove through villages where there were only solitary bulbs shining, powered by generators. In fact it was wonderful to have so little light and see the sky so clearly. Power cuts are the norm. We had two torches with us, purchased after much discussion, but they have paid their way already.

The bus driver prayed before we set out. Rob thought he would have done better to check his brakes. But he drove well, and we arrived in Kalemyo in time for our first square meal in forty-eight hours in a restaurant which was entirely staffed by children. However, this was because it was Christmas Day and all the adults were at church. They returned after midnight and welcomed us warmly. We got quite friendly with them over the three days of our stay – their English was excellent and they were happy to chat. Their views on their country were refreshing and they were not afraid to share their thoughts. They have five daughters, several of whom are in the United States, having achieved political asylum by travelling through Guam.

Toe, our guide, hired a minibus and we set off for a hill that overlooks the plain of Kalemyo, passing a checkpoint into Chin state. But we were only allowed to go for three or four miles. After looking at the view, we had to turn back.

Back in town we abandoned the car and set off on foot. Halfway down one street a guy on a motorcycle stopped us and asked Toe for our papers. We were not allowed to go any further down that street. The motorcyclist, obviously a policeman, then attached himself to us for the rest of the day. We walked, he rode. We stopped for a beer, he sat with us. At one point

Toe, the policeman and the trishaw driver were all sitting with us. Not much romance allowed here. The same trio had dinner with us, which of course we had to pay for. They say that all this security is for our own good. In other words, kidnapped foreigners can become international incidents. We were not particularly worried, just a bit claustrophobic.

Despite all this, we quite like Kalemyo. It is a wealthy town due to its trade across the border with India and we have seen the first plump Burmese, also the first Burmese to wear spectacles.

We visited Kalewa in an old pickup, very bumpy and dusty. We got filthy. At the fork for Tamu there were trucks fully laden heading for India. Others were Tiddim-bound via Kalemyo. All the houses, boats, scaffolding, even the scrap and firewood, are teak wood. Deforestation is rife. We have asked a couple of times about replanting programmes, with sketchy replies. Every piece of flat ground is planted with crops. Trees or vegetables? A conundrum for ecologists.

YE-U and SHWEBO, January 2003

The journey to Monywa was dull, as we had done it twice before, but we perked up as we turned for Ye-u. The road got smaller. We passed through a military town and after that there was nothing but paddy fields. Ye-u seemed fairly prosperous. We found the road to Kalewa where we had been three days before.

There is now a bridge over the Mu river which the Camerons forded at chest height. After the Mu the road turns to dust and we had a very long, bumpy and dusty ride. We are now among the plains people, who are mainly farmers, although the land belongs to the government. The river people, whom we had seen on our voyage up the Chindwin, seemed to have more of a hand-to-mouth existence whereas the hill people whom we met round Kalemyo appeared to be traders and more prosperous.

We arrived in Shwebo in time for dinner, a Chinese meal which we ate overlooking a lake accompanied by a hungry cat, a gecko, a dog, – oh and inevitably Toe and our driver, Nellie (a man!). We are staying in the dirtiest, dingiest place I have ever seen, but it's the best room in town, also, I would guess, the noisiest.

MYINTHE, January 2003

We've found it, hurrah! The exact place from which the Camerons crossed the Irrawaddy. We drove along the road to Monywa before turning south on what eventually became a dirt track. Passing through a village we turned towards the river. This took us to where the car ferry leaves for Ngazun. After lengthy discussion (and money changing hands), our guide arranged a fishing boat for us and gave us the happy news that Myinze and Myittha were five miles downriver and right next to each other. Off we set in the boat. Sure enough we came to Myinze first.

We got ashore and walked through the village. Everyone came out to greet us and by the time we were half way through we had accumulated in our procession all the local experts. One man, seventy-two years old, remembers the British in the village, which, amazingly, was not abandoned during the battle. Another remembered how the British helped them after the battle was over, gave the village a pump and taught them irrigation so they could water their crops. He also said that at really low water about February or March you can see the remains of a tank in the Irrawaddy. He told us about seven British soldiers buried in his field and took us to the place. Sadly the graves are unmarked. He tells stories of how 'this tree here' harboured a Japanese sniper and 'that path there' carried all the British down to the river once the heavy equipment could get across. We are now in Myittha, next to a monastery. The opposite bank of the Irrawaddy looks steep. To our right is Dawete, where the Worcesters were attacked by a Japanese cross-river raid. Opposite is Ngazun. We walked through the monastery in Myittha and stopped to talk to the monks who were in the middle of a school lesson. We were able to leave them pens. Then on through Myittha village. The locals have not seen any Western people since the war, but two Japanese have visited.

The headman of Myinze invited us all for tea. Unlike at Kohima we could actually imagine Dad and his company in both villages. Back into the fishing boat and for more money they agreed to make the crossing. Following Dad's diary we left from Myinze and turned down river to avoid the sandbank following it for a while and then turned around the end of it and heading for the steep banks opposite. We really felt we had achieved what we came for and our feeling of elation has lasted. We've taken 95 photographs today.

Chapter Eight

The Road to Mandalay

On the road to Mandalay,
Where the old Flotilla lay:
Can't you 'ear their paddles clunkin' from Rangoon to Mandalay?
On the road to Mandalay,
Where the flyin' fishes play,
And the dawn comes up like thunder outer China 'cross the bay
RUDYARD KIPLING

THE DISTANCE FROM NGAZUN TO MANDALAY is about thirty miles, the route following the south bank of the Irrawaddy upstream to the southern end of the great Ava Bridge, the central span of which lay in the river, demolished by the British during their retreat in 1942. The Japanese whom we encountered were fighting delaying actions to prevent the 2nd Division cutting their line of retreat south from Mandalay, on which Pete Rees's 19th Indian Division was advancing from the north.

Our quite rapid advance provided some textbook battles at company level. With my own artillery Forward Observation Officer, a troop of tanks and a section of machine guns temporarily under command, such engagements were heady stuff for a twenty-four-year-old company commander.

Near Kyauktalon on March 11, we were faced with a small ridge on which the Japanese were entrenched. We did not know that there was a deep dry riverbed between the hill and us. When we came on it, I sent Mike Spreckley with his platoon across it on the left, where the hill ran down towards the Irrawaddy. There they came under fire, not from the hill, but from the lip of the gully behind them to their right. I suggested through the telephone of the leading tank that it should move forward to the edge of the gorge to give us cover, my language deteriorating (as usual in moments of stress) when the troop commander hesitated. The tanks were operating with their turrets closed, possibly as a result of an incident a few days earlier when a Japanese had mounted a tank from behind and beheaded the commander.

As the remainder of D Company descended into the gorge, several fleeing Japanese revealed the point from which Spreckley's platoon had come under fire. We cleared the gorge, mounted the opposite bank and charged up the hill covered by machine-gun fire, finding some enemy dead in their foxholes, but most had gone. At this stage of the campaign, the Japanese did not fight as resolutely as they had at Kohima. They were in retreat and outnumbered. Some perhaps were new to combat.

That day we had a visitor, a middle-aged supply officer of the United States Army Air Force. He had requested a day 'at the front', and it was almost his last, since he cheerfully joined our attack. After sleeping the night with us, he returned to his base with a lot of souvenirs and some direct evidence that the 'shells and things we send up to you boys' were being put to good use.

The following day the Brigade advanced at a stroll, myself falling into step with the affable Mike West. A brigade advance across open country, infantry spread out, tanks in support, machine gunners and mortars ready to deploy, was a rare event in the Burma Campaign. On this occasion it was enough to scare the wits out of a small party of Japanese who had dug a shallow ditch, from which they turned and ran, leaving their neatly packed rucksacks. Obviously they had not been taught the art of retreat.

Compared with the wars of today, Burma in 1945 was a bow-and-arrow affair. At this stage of the campaign, the Japanese were increasingly desperate; the British remained stoical; the Indians, as ever, professional. One thing they all had in common was a lack of empathy with the people of the country in which they were fighting. The Burmese were a sort of backdrop to the war, indifferent to claims of being 'liberated'.

The 14th Army, beneath the surface of its clinical strategy for victory, was emotionally motivated by a need for vindication after the defeats of 1942; by a desire to avenge Japanese atrocities; and by faith in the righteousness of its cause. This was a recipe for war without mercy. Tens of thousands of Japanese in Burma paid with their lives for their commanders' folly. They were sent to their deaths, ill supported, with only their native courage to sustain them.

To the end of the campaign, in which the Japanese lost most of their 300,000 soldiers, they remained stubborn in defence; careless in attack; so unaccustomed to retreat that they waited till you almost tripped over them before they ran away; so bemused by capture that they were totally cooperative. I learned from British Intelligence Officers who interrogated Japanese prisoners that there was no stiff upper lip. They answered every question in detail and at length, perhaps feeling they were as good as dead, so what did it matter? They felt disoriented when they were treated humanely.

By March 20 we had reached Amarapura, a western suburb of Mandalay. We had alternated the lead since Ngazun with our comrade battalions, the Dorsets and the Worcesters. It had been a bit of a romp, compared with our earlier experiences, although not without casualties, and still with that casual proximity to the enemy which could be disconcerting. For example, as my Company occupied a village before dawn, a Japanese patrol marched silently past us down the main street, obviously having no idea that we were there. We were so surprised that we at first assumed they must be locals. Half an hour later we were heavily shelled and had four men wounded.

The following morning the Dorsets took up positions in the dark on a forward slope facing eastward. The dawn came, and the Japanese began to pick them off one by one. The Dorset platoon commander went out again and again to bring in his wounded, and was killed in the process. No memoir can do justice to such a sacrifice.

★ ★ ★

I was amused to read in Ian Swanson's diary that at this stage of the campaign he regarded D Company as 'too ambitious'. I suppose that is because I kept harassing Angus to let me advance faster, and sometimes he did.

Mandalay was a disappointment to us. The surviving Japanese had fled southward. Almost the first person we met was Pete Rees, the flamboyant Welshman who commanded the 19th Indian Division, identifiable by his red scarf below his bush hat. Whistling past us in his jeep to visit the Ava Bridge, now behind us, he called cheerfully 'Hello, Camerons,' a greeting we returned with reserve. We would have liked to have taken Mandalay.

The author (*left*) with Neil White at Mandalay, March 1945

Amarapura had its consolations. It was the only place in Burma where we received a welcome from the civilians, who were Indians, long-time residents of Burma. Hoarded rice was uncovered; gratitude was expressed. There were even a few garlands. Such warmth took us by surprise. Stan Mawdesley said to me: 'This man has invited us to his house for a meal, sir. Is it all right if we go?'

At the end of March we were trucked about forty miles southwest from Mandalay and then advanced on foot towards Mount Popa, an isolated peak famous for its temples and cobras, where the Japanese had taken up defensive positions. We were now in arid, treeless country with temperatures rising to 45 degrees centigrade.

As we advanced across the plain, we encountered a few forlorn groups walking towards us in twos and threes, waving wisps of white cloth. They were soldiers of the Indian National Army, victims of history, glad to be alive and get away from the Japanese. When the Japanese captured Singapore in 1942, Indian sepoys were separated from their officers and given the option of being prisoners of war or fighting alongside the Japanese. Later Subhas Chandra Bose, who was in Germany in 1942, was conveyed to Japan in a German submarine and took command of what became the Indian National Army.

The Mount Popa engagements were open warfare – no jungle, no villages. The country – apart from the temperature – was reminiscent of the Yorkshire moors on which the Division had trained in 1940 and 1941. The morning after we dug in within sight of the Mount Popa foothills, three carriers (tracked vehicles with mounted Bren guns) drove through our lines without stopping and down the hill under the Japanese guns, which knocked them all out, killing four of the crew and wounding four more. D Company was assigned to rescue the survivors. Our wonderful gunners blanketed the Japanese positions with smoke while our patrols brought in the dead and wounded. Why had the carriers done such a foolhardy thing? I couldn't ask Donald Mowat, the platoon commander – he was dead. We learned that he had been told to advance to a certain milestone – the one where we were dug in. He was at a milestone all right, but it was the next one. It was his first and last time in action.

At the beginning of May came the surprising news that the entire Division was to be flown to India. However, the 5th Brigade (Camerons, Worcesters and Dorsets) was then asked if it would please first capture the Mount Popa foothills. At this point Angus McAlester fell sick ('over-wrought' according to the Swanson diary), so Allan Roy, second-in-command, led the battalion in a series of company attacks over bare, rocky hillsides. Our last casualty before being evacuated was a Jock who was found dead. It was at first assumed to be a case of heatstroke. Only in the first aid post did they find the cobra bite on one of his legs.

Transport planes, manned by cheerfully relaxed American crews, took us to Chittagong, where we entrained for Calcutta. The gossip was that the Division would make a sea-borne landing to capture Rangoon. As it proved, Mount Popa had been our last engagement.

Footsteps 4

Excerpts from Sylvia May's Diary

MANDALAY, January 2003

*We were now on the main tourist track. Our goal of following the Camerons'
1945 route through Burma has proved to be very difficult to arrange. We had
been told by Emperor Travel in correspondence that some of the places we
wanted to visit were off limits. To reach others we would have to retrace
our steps. Burma wants tourists, but they are channelled into a diamond-
shaped itinerary with Rangoon in the south and Mandalay in the north. The
westernmost point is Bagan, and the easternmost is Inle Lake. Everything
else requires special permits and guides. But to get visas in the first place,
you have to book a tour. We are not very good at being tourists.*

*We got to Amarapura today, a pretty villagey suburb on the southern out-
skirts of Mandalay, which the Camerons entered from the west in 1945.
Visitors see a lot of temples. Today we also saw a silk weaving factory. Then
we went to the top of Mandalay Hill which now has escalators and a lift. It
commands a panoramic view of the city and the surrounding country.
The Irrawaddy snakes to the south before turning sharply to the west at
Mandalay. In the quiet sunset it is hard to imagine what happened here
fifty-seven years ago.*

*From the top of Sagaing Hill we had a fabulous view up the Irrawaddy and
of the Ava Bridge, photographing which is strictly forbidden, but I managed
to get a furtive shot through the car window. Back in Mandalay, we actually
got away on our own, walking down one side of the Fort, which houses the
army. We could have visited the palace for $5 each, but decided to conserve
our dwindling cash. We have already resisted purchase of silver when taken
to see the silversmiths of Sagaing. We went to Mingun and saw the Golden
Palace, which is not gold but exquisitely carved teak, which was once
painted gold.*

*All the cars here are Japanese, Mazdas for taxis, otherwise Toyotas and all
have right-hand drive, although they drive on the right. The only left-hand
drive vehicles are old Willis jeeps and the odd Landrover. The basic transport is bicycle or horse and cart.*

Emperor Travel took us out for a New Year dinner – a rooftop table, excellent Chinese food, including crispy duck. Then we watched street theatre – the kind of place where the Moustache brothers performed their political satire and got arrested for their pains.

We went to Maymyo in our guise as tourists, staying in the 100-year-old colonial-style hotel which must have been beautiful once. Now owned by the government, its staircases, balconies and grounds are sadly in need of renovation. We planned what we would do with it if we took it over. The only noise you hear at night is birdsong. Maymyo being famous for its strawberries and flowers, we walked around the botanical gardens.

We also had our first decent walk since arriving in Burma, a long one to the Anisikan Falls and it seemed even longer coming back. We have difficulty in getting into sync with the Burmese eating habits. They are big lunch eaters and we are not. So we have ended up eating two large meals a day. Snacks are unheard of. The trouble is that we are paying for lunches and dinners for our guide and driver and, boy, do they have appetites! The guidebook says that you can eat well for 1,000 kyats a day, but it is costing us 6,000 kyats – plus beer. Still, we have kept within our budget of 7,000 kyats a day.

Our walk today turned into an eight-person march. The five additional were local people who carried cold drinks, available for sale on demand. One of them pushed me up the hill and fanned me with her hat, which also turned out to be a commercial service. So the two-hour walk cost 1,500 kyats and put us over budget for the day.

MOUNT POPA, January 2003

This hotel is the place to be. Situated about one third of the way up Mount Popa above a hill with a pagoda on it, it is featured in all the guidebooks. The rooms are wooden chalets set into the hill. Ours has a fantastic view of the plains. The only down side is that we don't have enough money to enjoy such attractions as mountain trails, horse riding and bird watching. We have never seen such enormous spiders as there are here. Hundreds of them hanging on giant webs between trees. Rob went on a walk through the jungle and said how easy it would be to get lost.

On the way from Bagan we stopped several times to look at local industries based on the use of palm oil. One of these is a drink which is not alcoholic in the morning but by the time it has fermented in the afternoon tastes like medicine. They also make peanut oil, the grindstone drawn by oxen. It all looked like a rural idyll.

Rob set off early to climb Mount Popa. He was there and back in five hours – not bad for a 5,000-foot ascent. I spent the day on the balcony of our room or by the pool reading. This is truly a great place to rest, quiet and clean in wonderful air and amid beautiful scenery.

Although we could not follow all of the Camerons' 1944–45 route, at least we have finished where they finished.

Chapter Nine

Farewell to the Regiment

There's a long, long trail a-winding
Into the land of my dreams
Where the nightingales are singing,
And a white moon beams
There's a long, long time of waiting
Until my dreams all come true
Till the day that I'll be going down
That long, long trail with you.
World War I song

When this bleeding war is over
Oh how happy I shall be ...
World War II song

D AVID MURRAY and Dave Davidson lived near to each other in
their retirement years in the Scottish Borders. They would sit
together for hours ruminating over their wartime experiences, and,
David told me, had reached the conclusion that those who served
together in the 1st Cameron Highlanders during World War II
were an exceptional body of men.

This had not occurred to me. I thought of the battalion more as
a happenstance selection of the between-wars generation, blended
by shared experiences and welded by regimental tradition.
Compatibility was not a given. We were novitiates privileged to
have joined an elite institution. Pursuing excellence, to what end
we were not quite sure, we acquired an aura of pride, a feeling,
frankly, of superiority, through years of boredom, tension and
occasional peril. We would have been lonely without one another.
As a result, the whole was greater than the sum of the parts. We all
did better than we expected of ourselves. A bunch of young men
patriotically motivated, physically fit and geared for high endeavour,
had no choice but to live together for years. There was talk of discipline and duty, but without belief and shared ideals, it would not
have worked. When we were depleted by casualties and disease, the
core of this spirit remained constant enough to imbue incomers. As

in all military units, fellowship became a substitute for family. Feuds, quarrels and jealousies were subdued in deference to the common cause.

At the same time, there is some evidence that the Camerons did achieve an exceptionally high standard of morale in the peculiar conditions of the Burma Campaign. Roy McKelvie, himself a Cameron officer, who became a war correspondent, wrote in his book *The War in Burma* (Methuen, 1948) that '... those responsible for the maintenance of morale and efficiency ... were up against a wave of demoralization ... these facts may be hard to accept but they were found in the monthly intelligence reports submitted by units. Every month saw the same references to the growing depression among British troops. No attempt was made at the highest level to halt this process'.

The Swanson diaries, written in 1946, contain a reference to the 'sadly affected battle nerves of a neighbouring battalion'. During the campaign, I heard eyewitness accounts of what might politely be called precipitate retreat, and one about a soldier reporting sick with battle fatigue who, on entering the medical tent, saluted smartly, raised his rifle and fired a shot at the medical officer. Such anecdotes were regarded as gossip or aberrations to be hushed up.

A report by the divisional psychiatrist, written in 1945, threw a bouquet to the Camerons:

> It is an obvious fact that in any unit, apart from men who are manifestly unsuitable for battle conditions and should have been excluded by selection work previously, there will be an admixture of good, moderate, and indifferent soldiers, and it cannot be denied that psychiatric battle casualties are drawn from the two latter groups. I consider the breakdown in battle of a really good soldier who comes from a unit where morale is high to be a very rare occurrence. I would quote as an example the 1st Battalion Queen's Own Cameron Highlanders, from which unit a minimal number of psychiatric cases occurred in both the Division's campaigns. The spirit of the men in this battalion was typified by one soldier who, during the crossing of the Irrawaddy, sustained a severe fracture of the femur; he was carried several

miles down stream, was in the water for many hours and was finally brought to the MDS 24 hours after his wound occurred. Even as late as that he was found to be in perfect physical condition and was quite unperturbed and very cheerful. I maintain that it is quite exceptional for men of this calibre to break down in battle. They form the group of those who are in the forefront of every attack and remain steady under almost any circumstances.

Maybe we were a little bit special. At the time we knew nothing about other battalions. We were entirely self-contained. Even in long retrospect I have difficulty in explaining in what way we might have been different. Maybe our solidarity owed something to our distrust of authority. We were considered a tough bunch and did nothing to dispel this reputation. Cameron officers retained the loyalty of the wilder fringes of the Jocks with a mixture of visible discipline and tacit tolerance, and this paid off when we were in action. Off duty, we took it for granted that, if there was a brawl, some Cameron street fighters would be involved. Field punishments were meted out without malice, and received without rancour. The only unforgivable punishment would have been to get rid of these cheerful malefactors. There was a tacit rapport between the other ranks, who depended upon their NCOs to be their representatives, and the officers, who relied on the NCOs' advice. The wisest question a company commander could ask was: 'What do you think, Sergeant Major?' Most of the wartime officers, like the men we commanded, were city boys. We just happened to have gone to better schools. I recognized some of my Jocks from memories of the street-dwellers I had encountered in the Gorbals as I walked to school. Their attitude to life was to look for a fight. One of them, Private Chalmers, at the battalion's only reunion in 1972, reminded me about my bright idea of putting all the bad hats in the same section, with the thought that they would control one another, like a kind of street gang. 'We couldn't believe our luck,' he told me.

It would be inspiring, but untrue, to conclude that what held us together was conscious love of freedom and democracy – a desire to contribute to a better world – and if asked, none of us would have denied it. But our cement, and doubtless that of every unit in every army, was love of The Regiment. Like the French Foreign Legion, the fellowship came first, the cause second.

These reflections are prompted by my memory of flying out of Burma in the care of these genial American aircrews in May 1945. As I looked along the rows of Jocks seated in the big transport plane, I felt we were all in pretty good trim, battle-hardened ready for the next assignment. So when, in the succeeding weeks some of the Jocks, with passes to Calcutta, would wreck a restaurant or fight with other regiments (or with the Yanks), their officers were outwardly apologetic and inwardly relaxed. After all, we were waiting to go into battle again. The Japanese, however, let us down by evacuating Rangoon too easily, so there was no contested landing. All our practice at crouching seasick in landing craft and debouching dementedly onto bullet-swept beaches came to nought.

For some weeks we encamped on the banks of the Hooghly River, about twelve miles south of Calcutta. Peggy arrived from Bombay and we had a joyous reunion. We found a billet with the local police chief and there followed a blissful two weeks in the locality where Rumer Godden and her sister wrote their bestselling childhood memoir, *The River*, made into a film on location in the early 1950s by Jean Renoir.

On Saturday evenings, we would go dancing at the Saturday Club, known to its members, who were exclusively British, as 'The Slap'. Returning home from one of these occasions, I found my driver too drunk to drive, so I popped him in the back and took the wheel. There was a thunderstorm as we drove back to camp, which is my excuse for spinning the jeep into a deep ditch. I extricated Peggy, unharmed, barefooted, in her white evening gown, and gazed apprehensively at my driver, motionless in the back of the jeep, which had its front wheels in the air. But he wasn't dead. He was just unwakeable. We were towed out by some brother Camerons and the next day I listened gratefully to my Company Sergeant Major explaining to the MTO how a truck had dented the back of my jeep. We were a very close-knit bunch.

With the war over in Europe, reinforcements at all levels were arriving. The most senior was Sir Oliver Leese (ex-8th Army), who appeared one day at our camp to pin medals on Angus, Neil, me and several other Camerons. He did so without saying a word. We never did get to Buckingham Palace.

After two weeks we were moved to a remote jungle camp at Kamareddi in South India in preparation, it was rumoured, for sea-borne landings in Malaya. About this time the qualifying period for repatriation had been reduced from four years to three years and eight months, a political move in response to complaints from separated families, and perhaps not unconnected with the General Election which was to take place in July. Troops overseas were allowed to vote, and those in India, and no doubt elsewhere, voted unanimously against the government. Churchill was not a hero to serving soldiers who called Stalin 'Uncle Joe' and had no interest in the Empire.

If the invasion of Malaya had taken place as planned in September, few of those who had sailed with the convoy from Liverpool in April 1942 would have participated. Meanwhile, we old hands were asked to train new arrivals in jungle warfare. Most of them were apprehensive about exchanging the war in Europe for the war in Asia. We wrote a training manual which Colin Hunter wittily wanted to entitle *How Green was my Battledress*.

Not wishing to return on a troopship to the UK since Peggy was pregnant again, I wrote to a friend in the GHQ Public Relations Directorate in New Delhi and asked if there were any jobs going. My idea was to prepare myself for a future life as a newspaper correspondent. By my friend's kind intervention, I was posted to General Auchinleck's staff under the command of Brigadier Desmond Young, who was one of my heroes. He had commanded a battalion in World War I at the age of twenty-seven; spent ten years after the war salvaging ships all over the world; taken up journalism, first in South Africa and then in India, where in the 1930s he had revived Rudyard Kipling's newpaper *The Lucknow Pioneer*. He had been in charge of the Government of India's press relations when war broke out, but wanted to go on active service. Captured by the Germans in North Africa, he escaped to Switzerland from prison camp in Italy, and had been back in New Delhi since 1944. He was to achieve fame after the war with his biography of Rommel.

My departure from the battalion late in July 1945 followed a Sunday lunch in the officers' mess tent in our jungle camp, prior to which Angus had gone behind the bar to mix me a drink, which, under the circumstances, I could not refuse and unwisely swallowed at a gulp. After lunch I was hoisted into an open jeep, in which I managed to stand to attention by holding the canopy bar and was pulled through the camp by a riotous crew of Jocks, who lifted me into the truck which was waiting to take me to the railway station, and over the back of which, as it drove down the dusty road – thank goodness out of sight of the camp – I was thoroughly sick. In this undignified manner, I left a comradeship which had enfolded me for four and a half years.

I was leaving not only the Camerons, but the 2nd Division, a wider family as part of which the Camerons and other regiments had learned how moral stoicism in the face of mortal danger can be the cement of sanity. This gave our Burma Campaign sustained meaning and a way of justifying to ourselves – peace-loving, law-abiding citizens as we were – our temporary readiness to kill and be killed, to be both executioner and victim.

At the end of my fighting war, I had to admit (only to myself) that it had not been a totally negative experience. When the atom bombs were dropped on Hiroshima and Nagasaki, two weeks after we arrived in Delhi, I had mixed feelings. It did not seem a fair way to win a war.

Chapter Ten

Staff Wallah

I have never been in a country where the sense of the present is so strong, where the future seems so unimaginable (unlikely even) and where the past impinges so little.

PAUL SCOTT *A Division of the Spoils* (Heinemann, 1975)

NEW DELHI at the end of the war was a backdrop to the twilight of Empire. Its broad boulevards and grand buildings bespoke the confidence of British rule. Only the ubiquity of uniforms suggested there might have been a war somewhere. Other great cities of Asia – Tokyo, Shanghai, Hong Kong, Manila, Rangoon, Singapore, Jakarta – had been bombed or fought over. New Delhi, protected by its remoteness from any theatre of war, was the capital of a country whose people were either against or indifferent to the war, although its armed forces had been major participants. The comfortable seclusion of New Delhi was no doubt one of the factors which influenced Mountbatten to move his headquarters to Ceylon, which at least, having been bombarded in 1942 had some claim to be a war zone. Climate may have been a factor. Peradenya, in the hills above Colombo, with its tropical gardens, was and is an idyllic spot, even more remote from the sights, sounds and smells of war than New Delhi. Joe Stilwell felt ill at ease in his sweat-stained bush jacket on his few visits to Peradenya as Mountbatten's deputy. But from Mountbatten's point of view it was free of imperial bureaucracy and the awkward proximity of Wavell and Auchinleck.

I had not been to New Delhi before and had to change my mental gear rapidly. I became a very junior member of Auchinleck's staff, reducing my rank from major to captain, and was posted to the PR (X) Department, 'X' meaning censorship. This gave me a chance to read the dispatches of some famous war correspondents, but it lasted only two weeks. My only excitement was my attempt to suppress the news of Japan's surrender. A story announcing it reached my desk at 8 pm on August 14. I decided I had better phone Desmond Young, who was dining out. 'No, he can't get away with that,' said Desmond. But I suspect the correspondent sent his dispatch anyway. Censorship was over.

Simmering beneath the panoply of the Viceregal establishment were the British elite running the Indian Civil Service and the high-ranking British officers of the Indian Army all beginning to face the inevitability that India would soon be independent. Following the failure of the Cripps Mission in 1942 and the Congress-led rebellion of that year, Nehru, Gandhi and other Congress leaders had been tucked away in jail. They were now free and preparing to take over. Clement Attlee's Labour Party, now in power in Britain, with clearer vision than the Dutch, French, Portuguese and Belgian post-war governments, saw independence for India – a cause which Franklin D Roosevelt had frequently urged on Winston Churchill's unresponsive ears – as part of its programme.

The slow-motion dawning on British residents of India that their 200-year rule was drawing to a close was poignantly portrayed twenty years later in Paul Scott's tetralogy *The Raj Quartet* – televised as *The Jewel in the Crown* – which I read with admiration and recognition of many of the characters, including parts of myself. No writer about events of that period has portrayed so sympathetically the sincere belief of the British rulers in their own benignity, their puzzlement over their rejection, their predictions of disaster and their feelings of bitter vindication following the mass slaughter which attended the independence of India and the birth of Pakistan in 1947.

In August 1945, for a brief moment, India had been united by euphoria over the end of the war with Japan. But soon Indian politicians, writers and demonstrators in the streets resumed their calls for the British to 'Quit India', a demand to which British troops were only too eager to accede.

I saw my time in New Delhi as an opportunity to educate myself for post-war life. With the end of censorship, I became a press relations officer, writing dull stories about Auchinleck's visits to his beloved Indian Army. He bathed in the warmth of his receptions. The Indian Army seemed to be his whole life, but he struck me as a lonely and melancholy person, kindly but distant. I suspect that he was still suffering emotionally from his demotion by Churchill from the command in North Africa in 1942.

Peggy and I travelled extensively on writing assignments. One was to write a history of V-Force, the code name for British Burma hands who had stayed behind Japanese lines to spy and nurture the loyalty of the hill tribes. I interviewed many of the V-Force commanders, some of them in Peshawar, others near the Khyber Pass on the North West Frontier, where the British had learned the art of guerrilla warfare in the late 19th and early 20th centuries. Others I found in luxurious officers' messes on hilltops with views of the Himalayas. Among curiosities indicative of Indian Army lifestyle, I noted at one such mess table-lecterns set at each of the well-spaced places on the long mahogany dining table bedecked with the regimental silver. Reading material from the side-table consisted of journals such as *Field*, *The Tatler* and *Horse and Hound*. I felt transported to the days of 'the Great Game', when the North-west Frontier was the only combat zone in Asia and the Afghan hill tribes, regarded with a kind of respect not extended to the Japanese, were the only enemy. Inspecting the Frontier Force Rifles in Peshawar, Auchinleck asked a grizzled veteran: 'How is my friend the Faqir of Ipi?' referring to a notorious rebel chieftain. He would not allow me to report the question or the answer. My V-Force assignment resulted in a small book entitled *V-Force, The Phantom Army of Burma*.

Peggy and I were billeted in a Maharajah's mansion called Mandi House. When not travelling, I reported to an office adjacent to the Viceregal quarters. Desmond Young offered me a job in Japan as press relations officer with the British occupying force, but I declined because our baby was due in a few months. Bored with writing bland communiqués, I confided in Desmond my hopes of becoming a newspaper correspondent. Advising me that I should start at the bottom, he called Sir Francis Low, Editor of *The Times of India* in Bombay, and arranged that I should work there as an apprentice. How he squared this with military regulations, I do not know. We moved to a flat in Bombay, and I started my training by learning to set hot type in the composing room, where I was lathered in sweat all day and from where I returned home each night with a sore back from sitting hunched over a linotype on a backless metal stool.

One day Low was having difficulty in covering Hindu-Moslem riots in an area of Bombay known as The Round Temple, and had the idea that I might report on it. Riots, I discovered, are more frightening than battlefields. You learn to keep smiling. At one point, a seething crowd made way for me and I found myself face-to-face with a bloodstained police officer holding a smoking pistol. Assuming that I was someone in authority, he saluted. Looking as official as I could – although hatless, I was wearing a khaki bush jacket – I said that I was glad to see that he had everything under control, and nodded reassuringly when he gestured to an upper window from which someone was firing. Falling back on the time-honoured phrase: 'Carry on, Sergeant', which has rescued many platoon commanders from predicaments, I retreated thankfully into the crowd, who obligingly opened a channel of escape. Sir Francis didn't think much of my report, since I was not sure who was shooting at whom.

Riots such as these were precursors of the terrible slaughter that was to take place when Pakistan was created in 1947. At the beginning of 1946, hope and fear played equal roles in Indian politics – hope on the part of the Congress Party that independence was finally within its grasp and fear that Hindu-Moslem strife would give the British an excuse to postpone it once more. But Mohamed Ali Jinnah, who was to become the founder of Pakistan, was adamant. After a meeting between him and Gandhi on Malabar Hill in Bombay, Gandhi was asked how the discussions had gone. 'Mr Jinnah has a difficulty for every solution,' he replied.

When the time for independence came, Mountbatten, who by then was Viceroy, set a timetable for the handover of power which compelled the Congress leaders to accept Pakistan and led to the bloodbath they feared. Bombay, a cosmopolitan city, India's trade window to the West – first colonized by the Greeks around 500 BC – provided a commercial veneer over the underlying tension. British expatriate businessmen were resuming their pre-war lives, but were cannily taking Indian partners. However, the Yacht Club, the Gymkhana Club and the Breach Candy Swimming Club continued their exclusively 'European' membership. It was an odd mixture of aftermath and prelude.

Peggy and I were having an idyllic time. Bombay was where we had met. We lived in a luxurious flat. We had many friends. The war was over. I was learning my new trade.

On February 15, 1946 my life fell apart. We were preparing to go to the cinema one evening when Peggy's birth pangs began. I rushed her to the military hospital in Colaba, where she went into labour at 8.30. At 9.30 a nurse came running to the waiting room. Peggy was dying. I held her hand, stroked her brow, spoke to her, but she was gone. The baby had survived. The doctor had no explanation. The death certificate said 'syncope following parturition'. This unexpected bullet was too close. From that moment I became, and remained for long afterwards, a spectator of my own life, outward composure hiding an inner void.

Setting out the following morning to return to the hospital, I found the whole town in chaos. The Indian Navy had mutinied. Desmond phoned from New Delhi for any eyewitness reports. I had only to look out of the window to see British troops armed with pick handles attempting to storm a tent occupied by mutineers and being put to flight with a hail of stones. A world gone mad. Fatalistically, I rode my bicycle through the crowds.

At such a time, your friends save you. They took me in, told me I had to eat. I sat for hours at the piano playing hymns. After the graveside service, I asked that a bougainvillea, Peggy's favourite flower, should be planted over her grave. Forty years later, it was still blooming.

The mother of Peggy's closest friend, Molly Sheehy, brought the three-day-old baby girl home. As Peggy and I had planned, she was called Fiona. Desmond Young was a tower of strength and a model of compassion, flying me and Fiona to Delhi, where I arrived in time to witness the great victory parade, which, under other circumstances, might have been memorable, but which left me unmoved. Lady Young was about to leave for the UK by flying boat, a dignified way to travel, with about twelve passengers, seated at tables for four at which white-coated waiters served meals. Desmond booked Fiona and me on the same flight. We took off from a lake in Gwalior. The trip took three days, with stops at the mouth of the Indus near Karachi, at Bahrain on the shore of the Persian Gulf, on Lake Habbaniya near Baghdad, and on the Nile, where we disembarked to spend the night on a houseboat. The last stop before Poole Harbour, the final destination, near Southampton, was at Catania beneath Mount Etna, snow-capped against a blue sky. Fiona, by now three weeks old, took the trip calmly. Lady Young was an angel. At Poole, a launch took us across choppy water from the flying boat, with Fiona in a basket, to a grim grey dock on which Peggy's parents, her sister and my mother were huddled. It was four years, less one month, since the *Marnix* had sailed from Liverpool.

★ ★ ★

Of course, I was still in the army. Ordered to report to the India Office in Whitehall, I found myself (courtesy of the ever-thoughtful Desmond Young) promoted to Lieutenant Colonel in charge of public relations of the Indian Army in Britain, a post for which I had scarcely any qualifications. From a flat in Belgravia, I strolled each morning across St James's Park to an elegant Whitehall office with a mahogany mantelpiece and a large leather-topped desk and a secretary awaiting my dictation.

London was enjoying post-war euphoria. It was only seven months since the war had ended, and this was the first peacetime spring for seven years. All around, but somehow invisible to those who had lived through it, were the devastation of war and the austerity of wartime economy. Those who had suffered six years of the privation of war were contriving, with British *sangfroid*, to pick up where they had left off. They did not seem to notice the bomb craters, the ruined buildings and the general tattiness.

The Indian Army was intent on making a last great flourish, its British officers steeling themselves for an emotional farewell and its Indian officers welcoming promotion but facing uneasily the prospect of fighting against each other. Hindus and Moslems, uneasily bonded under the British, were about to become open enemies. My main task was to organize an exhibition at Bush House in Aldwych at the foot of Kingsway, a project for which I had a team of competent designers. I was not really in command of anything.

People have sometimes asked how I attained the rank of Lieutenant Colonel at the age of twenty-five, to which I reply: 'It was a fluke.'

On the appointed day, there were marches, guards of honour and large crowds gathered to applaud the commanders of the Burma Campaign. Slim, Auchinleck and Mountbatten were all there, resplendent in uniforms and decorations. In striking contrast was Emanuel Shinwell, Minister for War of the Labour government, a small bareheaded man in a shabby raincoat. I was a sort of doorman for the arriving VIPs, whom I saluted and invited to inspect the honour guard. I think it was the only time that Slim, Mountbatten and Auchinleck appeared together in public. I arranged a group photograph, but noted that they had little to say to one another. Auchinleck elected to watch a movie about the Indian Army; Slim chatted with the Gurkhas; and Mountbatten spent most of the time in conversation with Frank Owen, the editor who had run the SEAC newspaper.

Apart from this project, my duties were light. Angus McAlester contacted me and asked if I would like to stay in the army. I was complimented, but the thought made me look forward even more to my demobilization which was due at the end of June. Some of my contemporaries had elected to go back to university to finish their degrees. Neil went back to Cambridge. Vic Kilgour found a job with the Rank film organization. Kitty's husband, Peter Pinfield, got a job with the British Overseas Airways Corporation. I saw a lot of them, but I was poor company. I took up vegetarianism, continued to shun alcohol, spent evenings discussing metaphysics and espoused the cause of world government.

Fiona was safely in Glasgow in the care of my mother. I visited them whenever I could. I was haunted by a sense of guilt, particularly towards Peggy's family, who were kindness itself. I also felt uncomfortable with my glamorous life in drab socialist Britain. Being waved to the best tables in London restaurants because of my uniform and rank made me nostalgic for the basic life. My six years in the army had hugely widened my horizons, but also reaffirmed my adolescent values.

For demobilization, I travelled by train to a school hall in Guildford, where, along with hundreds of other discharged soldiers,

I was issued with a suit, a shirt, a pair of shoes and a grey felt hat. I recalled the reverse process in Strensall Camp six years earlier when I was handed a battledress, a pair of boots and a forage hat. War service finishes as it begins, with piles of clothing issued across trestle tables. I insisted on trying on my suit, much to the alarm of the tailor measuring me, who pointed out that there were ladies present. 'Tell them to look away,' I said.

There were a few formalities to follow – a letter of thanks from the War Office, my medals in a nice box, and a gratuity of £300, part of which I used to send my brother's widow on holiday to Devon, and the rest to buy a second-hand car which I gave to Peggy's sister and her husband.

A friend offered me a job as a publisher's representative in Bombay. I accepted, stored my army kit in my black tin box and flew back to that city of memories with one small suitcase. I was to spend the next ten years travelling in India and its neighbouring countries.

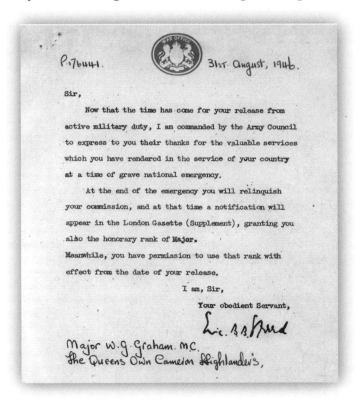

P.76441.   WAR OFFICE   31st August, 1946.

Sir,

Now that the time has come for your release from active military duty, I am commanded by the Army Council to express to you their thanks for the valuable services which you have rendered in the service of your country at a time of grave national emergency.

At the end of the emergency you will relinquish your commission, and at that time a notification will appear in the London Gazette (Supplement), granting you also the honorary rank of Major.

Meanwhile, you have permission to use that rank with effect from the date of your release.

I am, Sir,

Your obedient Servant,

Major W.G. Graham. MC.
The Queen's Own Cameron Highlanders,

Chapter Eleven

After the End

A soldier comes home in the immediate grip of experience, but it can take years – often a lifetime – to grasp what experience means.
VERLYN KLINKENBORG *International Herald Tribune*, 26 August 2004

M EMORIES ARE LIKE WILD FLOWERS. They seed themselves apparently by chance, not by human decision. They grow in inhospitable places and come in many varieties. They haunt our senses and appear in our dreams. Some are shy, born to blush unseen, the inward talks one has with oneself about things one has never told to anyone. Brian Aldiss, the science-fiction author, three of whose books reflect his Burma experience, told me that in his eighties he thinks about that time of his life every day.

Memories can also be aroused by unexpected meetings. Forty years after the end of the war I was attending the annual conference of the Booksellers Association at Aviemore in the Cairngorm Mountains of Scotland. I had parked my car at a beauty spot called Inshriach. As I returned to it, a voice from the next car greeted me by name. I had to say that I did not recognize the speaker. 'You should,' he said, 'we soldiered together long enough.' It was David Murray. We were in regular touch thereafter. David, having pursued a military career after the war, has a deep knowledge of regimental history and was the first person, outside of my family, whom I asked to read the manuscript of this book. He corrected a few memories, amplified others, supplied memories of his own and guided me to documents I had not known about.

Among these were the Swanson diaries. In the 1990s, an ex-Cameron, J R Lovelock, living in a village in Lancashire, discovered that a lady a few doors from him was the widow of Ian Swanson. Lovelock was seeking information about Angus McKay, killed at Kohima, on behalf of McKay's family. Learning that Lovelock had been in Burma, Mrs Swanson lent him her late husband's diary, which included several references to Angus McKay, who had been a close friend of Ian. This diary, copies of which are now deposited in the Cameron Museum in Inverness and in the Burma Campaign Memorial Library in London, is the only contemporary account of the Camerons' campaign, except for the Battalion's war diary, written daily by the Intelligence Officer, and understandably not a coherent account, although useful for place names, dates, map references and statistics. Seeing Ian's diary after I had written the first draft of this book was a poignant confirmation by a brother officer of many of my memories. I remember Ian, who was born in Buenos Aires in 1917 and had died in 1971, as a calm pipe-smoker with an earthy humour. Posthumously he emerges as a fluent writer and careful observer. He was Motor Transport Officer for the first part of the campaign. Arriving in Dimapur after the 2,000-mile, ten-day journey from western India, he recalls that he was greeted by Angus McAlester with, 'Where the hell have you been?'

In addition to his unpublished diary, Ian had supplied material on the 1st Camerons' Burma Campaign for the Regimental Records (Volume V), in which, however, the campaign occupies only thirty-six of 428 pages. 'Why is it so cursorily covered?' I asked David. He shrugged. 'We were seen as a side-show.' Kohima, he told me, was never mentioned in the Officers' Mess.

Fortunately, we have the written word as the treasure house of memory. Like many ex-soldiers, I was an eager buyer of books about the theatre in which I had served. Contemplating, fifty years on, my collection of about fifty books on the Burma Campaign, I fell to wondering where one might find a comprehensive collection of literature on the subject. The answer was nowhere. It was scattered over many libraries.

Between 1995 and 2000, with the help of fellow veterans, more than 1,000 books and manuscripts were assembled and presented to the School of Oriental and African Studies at the University of London. The Burma Campaign Memorial Library aims to enrich the memories of those who were there and inform those who were not, about what happened to the actors in that strange drama and also, incidentally, to reveal something of their ideals, their prejudices, their fears and their hopes.

About half of the books were contributed from personal libraries. The rest were purchased in the antiquarian book market or on the

Internet with the aid of grants from the GB Sasakawa Foundation under the auspices of the Burma Campaign Fellowship Group. The endpaper of each book carries a bookplate with the name of the donor beneath a drawing of cherry blossoms and a pagoda and a *haiku* about the continuity of life:

Blossoms fall to earth
The pagoda promises
That spring will follow

There is a bibliography divided into sections – Official Histories, General Accounts, Japanese Invasion, Arakan, Assam, Manipur and the Advance into Burma, China-Burma-India Theatre, Chindits, Clandestine Operations, Civilian Burma, The Gurkhas, Unit and Formation Histories, Autobiographies, Biographies and Diaries, Personal Narratives, Medical Services, Indian National Army, Newspapers and Ephemera, Journals and Newsletters, Pictorial Histories, Verses, Essays and Letters, The War at sea, The War in the Air, Fiction and a very few books by Japanese authors in English.

There are about 600 titles about the Burma Campaign written by Japanese authors in Japanese, about half of which are included in the Memorial Library. Unfortunately, the number of titles translated from Japanese into English or vice versa is very small. Only bilingual scholars can read accounts of the same events from both sides. The collections in both languages were duplicated in Tokyo and deposited in the archives at the Yasukuni war shrine – a site of which I disapprove, since it is a symbol of Japanese militarism. But I had to bow to the decision of the Japanese veterans.

Books about the Burma Campaign are still being written, more by historians, fewer inevitably by veterans, some of whom, in the twilight of their lives, are still seeking a redemptive message from these distant events. Were they just a black hole, a regrettable interlude, a tragic interruption in the pattern of their lives?

Some day, the Burma Campaign Memorial Library will itself be the subject of an historiography. At the moment it offers itself as a testament to the past and an opportunity for tomorrow. In the age of electronic communication, a book still remains the most deliberate and durable commitment on the part of an author, a time capsule of what he or she has experienced or learned and volunteered to share. In the hands of skilled librarians, a library lasts for hundreds of years. Some of the writings in the Library are unpublished memoirs written by old soldiers. At the time they are written, their letters and documents are of interest only to other old soldiers and the authors' families and friends. But for future generations they are the raw stuff of history.

In September 2004, the Memorial Library was exhibited to the public in Foyles Bookshop in Charing Cross Road. At the opening, Mr Ivor Caplin, Minister for Veterans, quoted Winston Churchill's statement that 'A nation that forgets its past has no future.' Mr Caplin's Ministry had chosen Kohima as the subject of the first in a series of booklets on major battles of World War II. At the Foyles opening, Viscount John Slim, son of the Burma Campaign Commander, and charismatic President of the Burma Star Association, spoke movingly of comradeship. Memory does not fade with age. Rather it sharpens, and seeks not only to distill messages dimmed by distance, but to refine them for future generations.

★ ★ ★

My younger daughter Sylvia, who was born in New York in 1957, and her husband Robert, are examples of next-generation pilgrims. Another example is Mike Sharpe, who was nine years old in 1944. Until he was six he had shared a room with his brother Dennis, who was called up in 1942 at the age of eighteen. Mike remembers the telegram coming: 'I said to my mother: "Missing?" "No," she said, "Killed." She went back into the kitchen'.

Mike kept all the letters his brother had written to him. When his parents died, he inherited the letters his brother had written to them. For the next fifty years, he never forgot his brother. In 1993, he joined a British Legion pilgrimage to Burma and found Dennis's grave in the Rangoon war cemetery. 'I cried,' he told me, 'but so did most of the others.'

He still didn't know how his brother had died. Research at the Public Records Office in Kew revealed that Dennis Sharpe had been one of twelve Royal Sussex soldiers killed at Hill 60 on August 5, 1944. That's a long way north of Mandalay in what is known as the Railway Corridor. Two visits later, Mike and a group of friends he had made on the first expedition got to Hill 60. On his fourth visit, he went there again with a veteran who had been in the battle and along with the daughter of a man buried next to his brother. Mike has become the leader of a group of veterans, widows and children of veterans who go to Burma and who have been pioneer visitors to many forgotten battlefields. In today's Burma, this takes courage and persistence, and testifies to their determination to keep in memory those who fought and died in a campaign overshadowed at the time by world events and now a footnote to history. Mike and his partner Joan are planning to take their children to see what Mike, seized as so many are by Burma's beauty and the gentleness of its people, calls 'the wonders of the Golden Land'.

Another remarkable pilgrim is Ellen Hannay, widow of one of the Camerons killed on their first day of action at Zubza. She had already become a camp follower by enrolling in the Women's Voluntary Service, and was not far away when he died in April 1944. She was within a few miles of Kohima on the day the war ended and walked all night to kneel by his grave at dawn. She has been back to Kohima eight times.

The brutally brief telegrams of death in wartime Britain (no counsellor came to the door), long after the shock of bereavement has abated, still leave the questions: how did he die and where is he buried?

I had a letter in February 2003 from an English *émigré* in Canada whose brother had been killed on the banks of the Irrawaddy in February 1945. That is all he knew. He had promised their dead mother that he would bring his brother's body home. Over the years, he told me, he had written many letters to 'the authorities', without response. Could I help him? He said that he was sure that if his brother 'had been an officer', the body would have come home.

I explained gently about Flanders Fields, quoted Rupert Brooke's 'Dust whom England bore, shaped, made aware' and assured him that no bodies came home from Burma, but that most of the British war dead there lay in carefully tended graves in military cemeteries. I gave him the address of the War Graves Commission. He thanked me from the bottom of his heart and said that his mother could now rest in peace.

The British have traditionally buried their war dead near to where they fell. Only during the Gulf and Iraq wars did the British public begin to see pictures of coffins being unloaded from aircraft and greeted by guards of honour and weeping relatives. We can guess that the dead don't care much, one way or the other. And although we who are left behind come to accept mortality as a part of life, it is hard to become reconciled to the death of those who die young – Jimmie Mitchell reaching for a hold on the Shelter Stone Crag; my brother Tommy, whose parachute failed to open; Arthur Woodall, Bill Kavanagh and Robert Moore-Hemsley on whom a fatal shell fell short; Arthur Carbonnel from his gangrenous wound; Willie Keir, bullet-riddled, holding my hand; Peter Barkey crouching in an assault boat; Angus Douglas and Joe Lyons, rescued by stretcher-bearers at least to die in company; or Peggy in childbirth – to name only a few from my small circle.

★　★　★

While the solace of memory comes to some through memorials and pilgrimages, for most veterans memories are maintained and revived by reunions. Comradeship is a great comforter. The Burma Star Association, while mainly a charity devoted to helping needy veterans and their widows, has for sixty years given Burma Star holders a sense of community, ever more precious as numbers dwindle.

In the 'Old Pals' Corner' of the Association's magazine DEKHO, the flow of faded photographs – not of macho warriors but of innocent young men in forage caps or bush hats – continues unabated sixty years after the campaign. Old friends are sought. New friends are made. The next generation, often knowing only vaguely that their fathers, uncles or grandfathers fought in Burma, seek to learn how they lived and died. The Burma Star has become a brotherhood. The Association used to fill the Albert Hall once a year, but its membership of 35,000 is now below 10,000 and the obituary lists in DEKHO get longer.

For twenty years after the war, I was not in the reunion loop because I lived in India and the United States. I had kept in touch only with Neil White and Vic Kilgour, more because we were kindred spirits than fellow veterans. In 1972 we went together to the only reunion the 1st Camerons ever held. It was a most un-solemn occasion. No speeches were made, no medals were worn, much booze was consumed. It reunited friends, but over three decades the collective comradeship of shared experience had dissipated. We had all gone our own ways.

After I retired from regular employment in 1990, I got a call from Colin Hunter, my old company commander, who had been secretary of the organizing committee of the Kohima reunion from its beginning. He was retiring. Would I fill the vacancy? I said I would be honoured, and sat on the committee for the next twelve years.

The Kohima reunion was one of the few held by a formation, as distinct from a unit, of the army. The 2nd Division, located in Germany after the war and headquartered in York for many years, generously extended hospitality and facilities to the veterans of Kohima over a weekend each July. To me, fifty years after leaving the army, the kindness and respect with which contemporary soldiers treated us ageing veterans was touching. Here was an institution which had not only maintained, but improved its standards. Regular soldiers of today strike me as modest, personable and articulate, as well as professional. Suddenly, I was proud to have been associated, however tenuously, with the army. When a youthful brigadier said to me 'You are our model,' I was at a loss for words.

The two-day programme at Imphal barracks in York each July has evolved over the years into a series of simple customs. On the Saturday, the garrison puts on a show for the veterans, their families, local dignitaries and citizenry. The Kohima Museum, a collection of artefacts regarded as a model of its kind by museologists, is open for the weekend. In the evening there is a dinner in the Officers' Mess and open house in the Sergeants' Mess. On Sunday morning a fleet of buses conveys the veterans and their families from the barracks to York Minster, where a small plaque commemorating the battle is set into an ancient wall on the periphery of the grounds.

The congregation sits in an arc on the lawn under the trees, facing the plaque. Preluded by mellow military music, the service of hymns and prayers is highlighted by a sermon, sometimes by a padre who served at Kohima – the late Gus Claxton of the Dorsets filled the bill eloquently – sometimes by a contemporary cleric, and, for the final occasion in 2004, by the Archbishop of York.

A veteran reads Pericles' funeral oration on the battle of Marathon. A young soldier reads *No Tears were shed at Kohima*, a poem written by a veteran. The presiding General reminds the assembly that the dead 'shall not grow old as we grow old'. The Last Post. Reveille. A veteran declaims the Kohima epitaph. A piper plays the lament *Heroes of Kohima*. Wreaths are laid at the plaque, sometimes by famous people – the Duke of Edinburgh in 2004. The national anthem.

After the service, the veterans are mustered in the cobbled lane behind the Minster by a stentorian no-nonsense Regimental Sergeant Major. There is a wheel-chair section, given gentler treatment. The band, playing, by request, at a slower tempo than usual, leads the march past the Minster steps. Crowds of tourists gather and applaud. The top-ranking guest takes the salute. The column files back into the Minster garden where the marchers give an eyes-left at the plaque before they disperse.

Back at the barracks there is a buffet lunch, and the bar does a good trade. After lunch, the presiding General (on the final occasion Major General Murray Naylor, who commanded the Division from 1987 to 1989) gives an address, which is followed by valedictions from Viscount Slim and the contemporary GOC of the Division, Major General Ian Loudon, who mentions, to a ripple of affectionate applause, the name of General John L Grover.

The British army does its music well. A Guards marching band plays selections culminating in the sunset ceremony and ending with *The Road to Mandalay* which, over the years, has become the Division's theme song. Rudyard Kipling's ghost must be pleased, if a little puzzled, by this resurrection of his famous barrackroom ballad, because the British soldier about whom he wrote longed to go back to Mandalay, while the 2 Div veterans never want to see the place again.

Only as the band marches off the tented square and Oley Speaks's setting of the Kipling poem fades into the distance, do my eyes mist over. It is sixty-four years to the day since I arrived in York as a raw recruit. I embrace the dozen Jocks who have mustered for this last hurrah and ask General Naylor's permission to fall out for the last time.

One Kohima veteran who does not hold the Burma Star was a regular attender at these reunions for their last twelve years. A small soft-spoken man, smartly suited below his panama hat, he was the guest each year of his close friend Maurice Franses, who had been a subaltern in the Norfolks at Kohima. Masao Hirakubo had been a supplies officer in the Japanese army. Conscripted in 1943, he soon found himself in Burma, and by April 1944 was the quartermaster of the battalion of the 31st Division defending Kohima village. He recalls with pride his achievements in improvising and delivering rations to the men of his battalion, for whom tough combat conditions were made worse by lack of a proper commissariat. The Japanese invading force was supposed to live off captured supplies.

Hirakubo's career ended in London, where he was manager of the branch of a trading company. Since he retired, he has made it his life mission to promote reconciliation between Japanese and British veterans, efforts which were recognized by the award of an OBE in 1990. In 2003 he asked if he could lay a wreath at the 2 Div plaque in York. His request was granted and after laying it, he said 'I am very happy'.

Hirakubo's mission has been intensely controversial. The attitude of the vast majority of British veterans to their quondam enemies ranges from indifference to detestation – mostly the latter. As we marched to the Minster gardens one year, Masao was taking photographs of the parade. A Jock behind me muttered, 'Japanese bastard.' The remark was made casually, without venom – a fact of life. Others feel more strongly. At a reception in the 1980s in London's Oriental Club, one of the last redoubts of British colonial tradition, chatting with someone who had been in Kohima in 1944, I raised the idea of a better understanding with our former enemies. 'I hate the bastards,' he said and turned on his heel.

Hate sentiments were commonplace during the war. The Swanson diary refers to 'little yellow bastards' and 'dirty little bog rats'. In the course of assembling the Burma Campaign Memorial Library during the 1990s, I had correspondence with British veterans about donating or bequeathing their personal collections to the Library. Some of them felt that the Library, which was defined as the literature of the Burma Campaign, should include books about the sufferings of British prisoners of war on the Burma-Siam railway. One of them felt so strongly about it that he refused to donate any books. He told me that he was quite unable to forgive and forget, and that he was content to be a racist as far as the Japanese were concerned.

British veterans' resistance to the idea of reconciliation with their former enemies is understandable in the light of the sufferings of the ex-prisoners of war who had to wait more than fifty years for compensation by the British government; who protested without avail at state visits to Britain by the Japanese Emperor, and who feel that the expressions of regret by the contemporary Japanese Government are not a real apology for the inhuman treatment of prisoners of war, and for many repulsive war crimes.

One can argue that the war crimes are no reason to hate the entire Japanese people for the rest of one's life, but logic is no match for deeply ingrained emotion. Even without emotion, it is hard to cross the cultural gulf between the two peoples, but a few have done it, notably Eric Lomax who wrote about his meeting with his former torturer in *The Railway Man*.

My own encounters with what came to be called the Reconciliation Movement began in 1984 when I had a message from Harry Seaman, who was at that time writing a book on Sangshak, the vital battle fought by the 50th Indian Parachute Brigade, in which he had served. A group of Japanese were coming to London on a mission of reconciliation. Would I like to meet them? In the course of several visits to Japan over the years, I had been too preoccupied with the business that took me there to make contacts, so I joined half a dozen British veterans and the Japanese visitors, who were being shepherded by Masao Hirakubo. British and Japanese faced one another stiffly over a conference table. Speeches were made. Cards were exchanged. I read and presented to the visitors a beribboned *haiku* I had written for the occasion. The Japanese seemed to be listening impassively, but, when we left, they lined up and embraced each of us.

I had long wanted to understand better these fellow human beings whom we had met under such unpropitious circumstances and into whom, during visits to Japan on business, I had achieved some insights. I had read numerous books about Japan, but neither through my reading nor my visits had I been able to connect the Japanese I met in Japan with those whom I had 'met' in Burma. I put this to my friend and colleague Riichi Inagaki as we walked among the bustling crowds on the Ginza in Tokyo in 1957. 'Riichi, I simply do not see in these people – smart, busy, polite – even a remote resemblance to the Japanese I encountered in Burma.' Riichi laughed. 'You were probably fighting farmers from Honshu and Hokkaido. The Tokyo regiments were too soft to be sent to the front.' I was not satisfied with that answer. I believed there was, or had been, a powerful military class dominating a fanatical fighting force, which in China, long before World War II, had established its reputation for ruthlessness and disregard for human values. On the other hand, the Japanese wartime army was made up largely of conscripts.

Riichi's own war experience was a commentary on this dichotomy. Shortsighted, bilingual, and well educated, he was totally un-military. Posted to the army's pay corps, he was captured by the Australians in New Guinea and spent four years in a prison camp in Australia, where he made one or two half-hearted attempts to commit *hara-kiri*. In 1947 he returned home, rather ashamed of having survived. His parents had already 'buried' him, and he has kept his gravestone for use when the time comes.

By the 1960s, I felt I had some insight into the Japanese character, but was confused between the older and younger generations. In their attitude to death, unquestioning obedience, their emperor worship, the older Japanese were absolutists. They did not seem able to think for themselves. Now there was a younger generation which seemed to be emancipating itself – somewhat.

During my time in New York, where from 1956 to 1963 I was International Sales Manager for the McGraw-Hill Book Company, I formed cordial relationships with Japanese businessmen of my own generation. They seemed to have dual personalities. One was in business, where their *modus operandi* was group-think. We never met them one-to-one. Decisions were slow. Meetings were formal. Laughter seemed to signify nervousness, not enjoyment. But when

you met them in the evenings, bathing naked together or dining in a Geisha house, they were, albeit self-consciously, more relaxed and natural. You never met their wives. You were never invited to their homes. The exchange of gifts was ritualized. Allegiance to the company was absolute. Once, when there was an error in quality control, the venerable martinet owner of our print company partner, lined up his managers and walked down the line slapping the faces of each one. Nobody resigned. But they were super-reliable as customers or partners and all worked like toads. Authority exploiting submissiveness? By the 1980s, I was still trying to link my peace-time impressions with my wartime experience.

My second opportunity for dialogue with Japanese veterans came in 1989 when Kay Kato, a colleague in Japan, kindly contacted the All-Burma Veterans Association of Japan (ABVAJ) and told them of my wish to meet some of their members who had fought at Kohima. ABVAJ is not a counterpart of the Burma Star Association. It was formed by the Japanese Government as a vehicle for arranging visits of veterans to Burma. Japanese battlefield pilgrimages are group expeditions performed as a sacred duty to their dead. I asked one veteran how he explained these mass pilgrimages to a country where the Japanese had suffered devastating defeat. He gave me a curious answer. 'You see,' he said, 'we are all Mongols.' I think he was referring delicately to the end of western imperialism in Asia.

About twelve Japanese veterans entertained me to dinner in Tokyo on the 1989 occasion, led by the redoubtable Major Nishida. They had all been back to Kohima since the war and were remarkably well informed about the battle. They brought maps and a large panoramic photograph of the Kohima Ridge. Only one spoke English, so conversation was slow, but they were urbane and relaxed. We were like a bunch of old friends exchanging reminiscences. Nishida and I agreed amid much laughter that we had probably thrown grenades at each other. They seemed to bear no grudges and to be philosophic about defeat. They saw no rift to heal, and nothing for which to apologise. Indeed, there is no word for apology in Japanese. It was a charming evening.

I wondered, however, whether the Japanese veterans of World War II are today an isolated group, detached from contemporary Japanese society. British veterans, sixty years after the Burma Campaign, are regarded by their fellow-citizens with respect and affection. The contemporary Japanese have long been freed of the fanaticism which motivated their parents and grandparents in World War II and appear to have blocked out of their minds the atrocities that Japanese forces committed against Chinese, American and British prisoners in the 1930s and 1940s.

Yet beneath the urbanity of the Japanese war generation, there is deep emotion. Visiting Tokyo in 1999, I learned that no fewer than 300 members of the ABVAJ were in Rangoon. Their mission was to mark the move of a Japanese cemetery to a new site. In their reverence for their dead, Japanese veterans had visited even remote areas in Burma, including those where the locals had no reason to welcome them. In Pascal Khoo Thwe's book *From the Land of the Green Ghosts* (HarperCollins, 2002) the author deals extensively with the death beliefs and practices of his people, the Padaungs, a Burmese hill tribe who fought against the Japanese. He tells of a visit by Japanese veterans to a village where their comrades had been tortured before being killed. The Japanese dissolved in tears as they heard descriptions of these deaths, but afterwards they and their Padaung hosts were reconciled over libations of rice wine.

The movement towards reconciliation began in Britain in the late 1980s when Royal Welch Fusilier veteran Gwilym Davies, angry at the unwillingness of many of his fellow-veterans to adopt a Christian attitude towards their past enemies, approached the Japanese Embassy in London to suggest that something should be done to 'heal the wounds'. This led to his introduction to Masao Hirakubo, who accompanied Davies on a self-financed visit to Japan to meet Japanese veterans. On his return, Davies was ostracized by his BSA branch.

As an outcome of this initiative, a group of like-minded British veterans, which included David Murray, got together to form the Burma Campaign Fellowship Group, (BCFG) with Masao Hirakubo as counsellor. Over a period of ten years, under its two chairmen, first Major General Ian Lyall Grant[1], who had fought with the 17th Indian Division and secondly John Nunneley[2], who had fought with the 11th East African Division, the BCFG arranged meetings, missions and services in the UK, in Japan, in Rangoon and in Kohima. The BCFG never had more than 150 members. It was dissolved in 2002 because it was felt that it had made its point and that it should be judged by its message, not its numbers. It offered a handclasp over walls of cultural prejudice.

The last act of the BCFG was to consecrate a plaque in the garden of St Ethelburga's Centre for Reconciliation and Peace, the mediaeval London church which was blown up by an IRA bomb in 1992. The message on the plaque reads, 'Yesterday's Foe is Today's Friend'.

The Japanese veterans retain a quiet determination that their footprints in Burma will not be forgotten. Even at Kohima, where there are no Japanese graves, although thousands of Japanese died there, there is a memorial discreetly erected by the Japanese in 1999. It stands on a hillside overlooking Zubza, the furthest point of the Japanese advance. 'This memorial stone-pillar,' it reads, 'is constructed in honour and memory of the Japanese soldiers who laid down their lives for their great Nippon during the Second World War at Kohima, Nagaland. We the Nagas remember the Japanese people and their country.' The memorial adds that the

---

1 Author of *Burma: The Turning Point* and *Burma 1942: The Japanese Invasion*
2 Author of *Tales from the Kings African Rifles* and editor of two volumes of essays by British and Japanese veterans

land is donated by Jotsoma Village and was constructed and inaugurated by the Naga National Council. Not all memorials celebrate victory. From the Japanese point of view, Kohima is their Gallipoli.

In Japan there are no remembrance services, no parades, no anniversary celebrations with media coverage. The shrine at Yasukuni is a controversial place, seen by most Japanese as a symbol of past militarism. Japanese war memories are concentrated on respect for their dead, which is not controversial. Former enemies, whatever their feelings towards each other, are united when it comes to honouring their dead. We all weep at graves.

A sad irony of the war in Burma is that both sides regarded themselves as liberators of a country which since then has become one of the world's most rigid military dictatorships. Defeat in war turned Japan into a democracy. Imperial withdrawal deprived Burma – so far – of its hopes of democracy.

Fifty years after the battle my wife and I entertained a party of fifty Burma Campaign veterans, Japanese and British. We finished the evening with a singsong. Two British octogenarians, dancing a soft-shoe shuffle, sang *Underneath the Arches*. The Japanese had brought the music for *Auld Lang Syne*, with words in Japanese. We sang it, holding hands, in both languages. When you can sing and laugh and cry a little with those who were once your enemies, you know that the war is really over.

★ ★ ★

At Pherima, near Kohima, there was found recently the headstone of a British medical officer who had died of his wounds, not in 1944, but in 1880, when there was a battle at Khonoma following the death in combat with the Nagas of a British political agent at Kohima. According to Verrier Elwin's *Nagas in the 19th Century* (Oxford University Press, 1969), the battle of Khonoma was the last organized Naga resistance against the British and was 'the severest fighting ever known in these hills'. Soldiers on both sides who participated in the battle of Kohima in 1944 might question this statement. Whatever the verdict, the Nagas, who had fought against the British in 1880, were stalwart allies in 1944. In 2004, the villagers of Khonoma marked the 125th anniversary of the last battle between the Nagas and the British.

Also near Jotsoma can be found emplacements used by the Nagas in their armed revolt against Indian rule in the 1950s. These relics remind us that every war reflects a human affliction that runs through history, and the memory of every war can become an instrument of healing, even if it takes generations.

This thought was in the minds of the committee organizing the Kohima reunions when they prepared for their last event and discussed what, if anything, could be done to perpetuate the memory of the battle after the reunions ceased. The outcome was the formation of the Kohima Educational Trust. In January 2005, my wife Betty and I, along with my daughter and son-in-law, Sylvia and Rob, visited Kohima on behalf of the Trust. This once-obscure mountain village is now a jostling, jumbled city, its narrow, twisting, ill-paved streets crammed with honking cars, mini-taxis and lorries; its buildings – from hundreds of flimsy shacks to the grandiose new police headquarters on Jail Hill – clinging precariously to the steep hillside. At its centre is a quiet, beautiful place, a garden set in a series of immaculately groomed terraces, where the citizens and their children go to relax, chatter, stroll and contemplate.

Whoever took the inspired decision to locate the Kohima War Cemetery on the ridge below and above the fateful tennis court, delineated now in stone, established not only a fitting resting place for the dead, but a haven for the living. The dead are embraced in the community.

They are, in truth, part of the community and of a wider community, if only we could see beyond the mists of mortality. As we paused over the Camerons' graves, I told Pfelie Kesiezie, our Naga host, how some of them had been killed, and what kind of people they were. He said that he had visited the cemetery many times, but had not been able until now to picture any of the men who lie buried there. Of the ninety-six Cameron names engraved on the memorial, only sixty-four appear on gravestones. The others were either never found or their remains lie beneath stones that say only 'Known to God'.

The Nagas do not have cemeteries. Their graves are everywhere. When you die, friends and neighbours immediately congregate at your house, whatever the time of day or night, and keep continuous vigil. The simple coffin is made and you are buried in your garden, or at the nearest available spot, with the result that you are remembered as an individual in the place where you lived. None of the Japanese have graves. Their comrades return still in the despairing hope of finding some bones to take back to their homeland.

Pfelie and I conjured a vision of photographs and brief biographies of the 1,421 British, Indian-Muslim and Gurkha soldiers buried there, and of the 917 cremated Hindus whose names are also recorded. Most of the dead were in their early twenties. Pfelie, who is a thoughtful philosopher, said he would like the twenty-year-olds of Kohima today and in the future to be able to picture those of their age brought to Kohima by the fortunes of war, only to die there. In 1944 these young men, British and Indian and Japanese, and the Nagas who lived here, were the victims of history and of miscalculations in high places. Japan's General Renya Mutaguchi, sequestered in his headquarters at Maymyo, tending his orchids, had overridden the doubts of his subordinates and overcome the doubts of his superiors. His hubris led him to believe that his troops could invade India and change the course of the war. On the British side, General Bill Slim did not realize that the Japanese 31st Division under the command of General Katuko Sato (one of the doubters) would or could make a lightning thrust across roadless mountains to Kohima. When the Japanese advance began early in March, General John Grover commanding the 2nd Division, offered participation, but was told it would not be necessary. If his offer had been accepted, the 2nd Division could have occupied Kohima before the Japanese arrived. As it was, a few hundred Royal West Kents and Assam Rifles were left to face an entire Japanese Division. The first 2nd Division units reached Dimapur on April 4; the Japanese occupied Kohima Village on April 5. If the 2nd Division had arrived two weeks earlier the outcome would have been the same, but fewer would have been killed.

Returning to Kohima sixty years after the battle, I reflected that no one could grasp the severity of the 2nd Division's task or the virtuosity of its performance without going there. 'Steep jungle-covered hillsides' does not convey the sheer physical intimidation of striving up them to confront an entrenched enemy. There are no flat places. To those below, the landscape towers. The British victory was a stupendous feat of arms.

To those on the high places, the hills roll to the skyline, affording psychological as well as physical assurance. But who would wish to choose between dying in a bombarded foxhole or while charging a nest of them? The Japanese sacrificed their young conscript troops through repeated frontal attacks. One nineteen-year-old Japanese soldier apologized to his officer for dying. Their courage was wasted.

British books about the battle record what the Nagas did in those epic days, but not what they thought. The elders of Kohima Village, red-blanketed, barefooted, wizened, clutching their wooden flagons of *zu* (rice beer), told us their stories. The Japanese had assumed that the Mongoloid origins they shared with the Nagas would ensure them a welcome, but even when this argument was acknowledged and expressed in hospitality, the Japanese sacrificed goodwill by their rapacity. The villagers of southern Nagaland, who had initially welcomed the Japanese, watched them silently in their pitiful retreat. The Nagas of Kohima had no doubts from the outset – their hearts were with 'the Whites' – a loyalty attributable in part to one hundred years of proselytization by American Baptist mission-aries and in part to Naga loyalty to the British administration ever since the bitter British-Naga war of the 1870s – a loyalty, however, dissipated by the British handover to India in 1947.

Naga history is oral. The elders' war stories are dying with them. Some of the new generation still have childhood memories. The Nagaland Minister of Education told me that he remembers being taken away at the age of eight from Kohima Village by his mother on April 4, 1944. The family lived in the jungle until the end of June. Their house, which stood on Church Knoll, was totally destroyed. Pfelie Kesiezie confirmed Masao Hirakubo's story about the destruction by British gunfire of the granaries of rice so badly needed by the Japanese. They belonged to his grandfather. We met also Easterine Iralu, a writer who is gathering the wartime memo-ries of the Nagas into a book.

After the battle, British Army engineers helped the people of Kohima to rebuild their houses and also built a new hospital on the spur below Garrison Hill and a secondary school near Merema, structures which have weathered well the sixty years since they were built. But after 1947, communications between the British veterans and their Naga allies were scarce and spasmodic. British Legion missions to Kohima, squired by the Indian Army, concentrated on their own memories. Meetings of British and Japanese veterans devoted themselves to acts of reconciliation. Kohima was a place, not a people.

But when the ageing British veterans contemplated their last reunion their thoughts turned to the people of Kohima. There should, they felt, be more than graves and memorial stones to remind those who live in Kohima now, and those who will live there, of the part played and the price paid by their ancestors in a war not of their making. This letter was sent to all Kohima veterans:

'2004 will be the sixtieth anniversary of the battle of Kohima. Since 1950 veterans of the battle, along with their friends, families and contemporary members of the 2nd Division, have met annually to commemorate the comradeship of all who served at Kohima and the sacrifice of those who did not return.

'Next year will see the last of these reunions. This raises the question: Should the memory of the battle henceforth be enshrined only in memorials, on gravestones, in our fine museum at York and in the history books? Or is there more that could be done to keep it alive and give it meaning in the minds of future generations?

'There is a positive answer – one in which we can all participate. It springs from the obvious fact that Kohima, which we remember as a battle, is actually a place where people live. The Nagas of Kohima and other villages were our staunch allies during the battle. They served as guides, spies, porters, stretcher-bearers and combatants. They suffered casualties. Their homes were destroyed. Without their aid and support, the battle might not have been won. As one Naga said: "We were like brothers." The Nagas received much praise and gratitude, but that was long ago. For nearly sixty years there has been very little contact between the veterans of the 2nd Division and their Naga allies.

Now, with the ending of our reunions, we have the opportunity to recognize and renew the bonds of friendship forged in battle.

'So was born the Kohima Educational Trust. Its purpose is to help Nagas with the education of their children in any ways appropriate and possible within the Trust's means. The Trust plans to achieve its goal by means of scholarships, exchange visits, awards, prizes and the provision of educational materials. For example, there is a serious shortage of schoolbooks in Kohima. Our first project and target is to establish a central library of books, chosen by the teachers of Kohima.

'As we consider what support we can each give to the Trust, we all naturally ask ourselves: Why should we support this particular idea in a world crowded with appeals for donations? The answer is that it is a debt of honour. Our friends in Kohima, a name immortalized in the history of warfare as one of the turning points of World War II, have needs which we can help to fill. Perhaps the best answer to the question is the reaction of a leading Naga citizen in Kohima in a letter to one of our Trustees: "You have not forgotten us."'

Within a year, £30,000 was contributed, mainly by veterans and the contemporary 2nd Division. Support from a wider constituency doubled this amount in the following year. A new generation of trustees, some of them children of veterans, are now developing the Trust. Pfelie Kesiezie, chairman of the Trust in Kohima, brought a group of Naga children to England in July 2005. The Trust's first projects – the schools' reference library, an essay competition, scholarships, and a teachers' seminar – are now under way.

★ ★ ★

On 14 August 2005, sixty years to the day since as a neophyte in Delhi, I had hesitated over a dispatch announcing the war's end, a splendiferous celebration of that historical moment was held in the grounds of Blenheim Palace. It attracted 30,000 people to watch vintage World War II planes fly past. Vera Lynn, 'The Forces Sweetheart', who had visited the Burma front, was there. So was a Glenn-Miller-type band playing for jitterbugging couples dressed in the style of the 1940s.

One small exhibit, organised by Rob and Sylvia May, and supported by three generations of trustees' families, traced the long road from the tree-blasted Kohima Ridge of 1944 to this celebration in one of England's grandest tree-blessed estates. The exhibit sold Naga handicrafts and books for the benefit of the Trust, and displayed maps and battle relics borrowed from the Kohima Museum in York.

The young and the very young paused to learn about Kohima – the place and the battle – for the first time. Some sixty-year-olds sought guidance in tracing the fate of relatives and friends. A few old men stopped to ruminate in silence. This confluence of generations on an historic English sward seemed to portray a moment to pass to the next generation the exploration of how war and memory can not only honour those who fought and died, but speak to those born long after the event.

Homage to the dead inevitably means most to those who knew them. Mourning is personal. When those who came home have lived their tomorrows and have fulfilled their obligation to tell 'them' about those who 'gave their todays', they too will live only in memory until they merge into history.

But ideas and ideals remain. That is why the end-of-war memorial service at the Cenotaph, organised by the BSA, seven days after the Blenheim event, conveyed beneath its solemnity a sense of farewell, but not of sadness. Octogenarians know how to enjoy the moment. All the symbols of life-continuity were there: music – military and sacred; colours borne by straight-backed, white-gloved veteran standard-bearers; hymns and prayers; leaders of church and state; the royal family in the person of the Prince of Wales, who led the wreath-laying. Television commentators at last gave the long-ignored Far East Prisoners of War the recognition and respect they deserved.

As the veterans strolled down a sun-dappled Whitehall to Parliament Square, the crowd rippled applause. The Prince of Wales circulated genially among the thousand Burma Star veterans assembled in Westminster Hall. Finally, the Forgotten Army had its own parade on a national stage.

Epilogue

SOMETIMES A FEW WORDS, simple inscriptions on memorials or gravestones, can speak volumes. The Kohima when-you-go-home war memorial is famous for the poignancy of its epitaph. Its words have been the theme of hundreds of remembrance services, including a few at Kohima, which, however, is too remote for all but a few British veterans to visit. I was fortunate to find myself in the vicinity of Kohima ten years after the battle. I had given little thought to the war since it ended. Veterans' children often say, usually after their fathers have died, 'He never talked about it'. This is not necessarily because the memory is bottled up. Life moves on. Living in India for ten years after the war, I was out of touch with my ex-comrades. I had re-married. Friedel, my Swiss wife, was a wonderful mother to Fiona, who at the age of three, had flown back to her birthplace, this time in the care of an Air India cabin crew. I was immersed in my work as a newspaper correspondent and publisher's representative.

Now here I was, by chance, within 100 miles of Kohima. I resolved, on what I thought was a whim, to go there for the week-end. At Dimapur, as I queued to get on to the public bus to Kohima, I was forced to define my mission when a military police-man stopped me. 'You can't go to Kohima, sir. There's a war going on.' 'That's funny,' I said. 'There was a war going on the last time I was there.' This time the war was between the Nagas seeking independence and the Indian Army enforcing the incorporation of Nagaland into India. I explained to the policemen that I wanted to do honour to my dead comrades. He let me go.

That weekend I rediscovered the power of place to evoke memory. It was an uplifting experience. I wrote it down on the second evening, without thought of publication. After I got back home to Bombay, I sent it to Vic Kilgour, who was by this time a successful surveyor living in the leafy exurbs of Surrey. He sent it to a friend on *The Times*, which published it anonymously, providing, unbe-known to me, a guessing game among Kohima veterans. The piece lay dormant for the next forty years until I showed it to John Colvin who asked my permission to reprint it in his book *No Ordinary Men*.

In my solitary weekend of impulse, I had unwittingly become a pilgrim. Of all the spurs to memory of a war, none can equal visiting a battlefield. Widows seeking graves, children seeking to see where their fathers fought or died, tourists seeking thrills, military historians seeking authenticity – all are moved by standing on the soil where mortal combat took place. For the returning soldier, a battlefield pilgrimage is like revisiting childhood, when values were simple and happenings were vivid. We make pilgrimages with the idea of mourning and receive instead intimations of immortality, which, we then realize, are what we have really been seeking.

I had no deep thoughts about trees when I wrote my piece in 1954 – only that they had healed the scars on a shattered landscape. I certainly did not dream that my rumination would provide the theme and title of a book fifty years later.

★ ★ ★

KOHIMA 1954

THE TREES ARE ALL YOUNG ON GARRISON HILL, and in Naga Village children are playing. The wet earth and sprouting shrubs have the same spring-fresh smell. And there is no stench. Grass-filled fox-holes still mark forgotten fire-lanes. Some rusty ration tins and leather straps have escaped, as too worthless to pick up, a decade of scavengers.

Beneath the Hill lie the graves. One thousand, three hundred and eighty-seven of them, in orderly, impersonal, endless rows. In this geometrical panorama there is no heartbreak, no rebuke, no regret. It is a design of peace, the pious peace that follows war, the revulsive peace of 'Never Again'. It is the mute attempt to express the inexpressible by those who, helpless, are left behind. It has the same conscious inadequacy as the 'Remarks' column in the Visitors' Book, where a sudden embarrassment catches the pen which has written smoothly the name and address and then stumbles on to an anticlimactic 'Very impressive' or, 'A fitting resting-place for heroes.' But one ex-soldier had written in a flash of perceptiveness, 'I wish my name were here.'

Yet the heartbreak is there. On this bronze plate or that is written the parting message of those who loved. Some are inspired; some are simple and heartfelt; some are superstitious; some, like the blank spaces in the Visitors' Book, are stifled to silence by the despair of incomprehension. But, mute or vocal, all concern those who speak, and we are left wondering what may be the response of those who are gone before. Do they know too much to keep their treasures in the crumbling storehouses of memory? Or do they go on unforgetful, yet untrammelled by past happiness?

> Killed in Action. 18 April 1944. Aged 27. 'Good Night, Daddy'.
> Killed in Action. 21 April 1944. Aged 29. 'A very parfit gentil knight'.
> Killed in Action. 5 May 1944. Aged 35. 'Beatae memoriae; quis nos separabit?'.
> Killed in Action. 6 May 1944. Aged 23. 'Our only beloved son, who died that freedom might live'.

Statistics can be comforting. Fifty thousand rupees, 200 saplings; 36 tons of cement; 1,387 graves, and 10 years. Like the poignant milestones, past which the country bus had driven in as many minutes as the advancing troops had moved in days, these figures measure the thinker, not the thought. To some they are mere computation; to those who were there they are the sight, smell and touch of a forgotten battlefield. Just as, at the summit crossroads where the bus groans to a standstill, the level space above is to some that which was once a tennis court and is now a war cemetery; to others it was a point of dominating destiny. Behind lies the tortuous mounting road. Before lie the jumbled blue forests and hills of Burma. Above the crossroads is the memorial, its message unread by those who pass, but commanding and holding the gaze of those who arrive:

> When you go home
> Tell them of us and say,
> For your tomorrow
> We gave our today.

On the memorial too, is written the story 'In March, 1944, a Japanese army invaded India ... at Kohima, it was halted, defeated, and turned back ...' In Rangoon a little while ago I met a Burman who had been living in the Chindwin Valley at that time. He saw the Japanese retreat. He didn't know much Japanese, but he always understood when the Japanese said the word 'Kohima' for then they would say nothing, only shake their heads.

Round the memorial are written the names. Brigadiers and privates; tank-drivers and stretcher-bearers, signalmen and riflemen; names from every corner of England, Scotland, and Wales. For our tomorrow, they gave their today. One of tomorrow's children guided me to the memorial on the Naga Village height. With proud knowledge he explained the bullet-riddled sheets of corrugated iron. The track which the bulldozers drove up the hillside is now a leafy lane; and houses identical with those which the battle obliterated have hidden the pattern of war till it can no more be traced. Red-blanketed Nagas, cheerful rebels now as then, stared in unbelief as I panted upward behind the nimble barefoot urchin to the place which I should have known better than he and which I knew before he was born. The Highlanders' memorial is in a houseyard, a confusion of fencing, pigs and hens. McCassey, Mackay, Mackinnon, Macmillan, MacNaught, in bronze alphabetical permanence. Here 88 were killed and eight were missing. Beneath the names is the title of the Cameron lament, 'Lochaber No More'.

The wail of the bagpipes from the Assam Rifles barracks on the ridge below was almost too timely a background to reverie. So, too, was the bugle sounding reveille when, stumbling through the thickets in the mist of a rainy dawn, I looked for ghosts and found none. We are the ghosts, called forth by our own memories, investing each impersonal inch of soil with our own personal meanings; these meanings our self-conjured mists in which, wraithlike, we startle only ourselves.

But as the mists are swept clear of the heights above by the rushing winds of an oncoming monsoon, there, where we stare uncomprehendingly at the sudden call for vision – still too sudden, too fleeting, but unutterably certain – is the great meaning we seek. For the trees are all young on Garrison Hill, and in Naga Village children are playing.

ACKNOWLEDGEMENTS

I would not have written this book if my daughter Sylvia and her husband Robert had not conceived the idea of touring the battlefields of the Burma Campaign. It was an arduous journey made during their vacation time and at their own expense. Their enthusiasm has been an inspiration. I would also like to thank Robert and our friend Bob Allen for long days spent at the Public Records Office digging out original documents, including the Camerons' war diary.

I could not have completed this account with confidence had it not been for David Murray, passionate soldier and thoughtful friend, who complemented and, where necessary, corrected my memories.

The memoir in its early draft was read and improved and encouraged by numerous veteran friends, including Allan Roy, Peter Grant, Rex King-Clark, Frank Cole, Maurice Franses, Keith Halnan and John Nunneley. A journalist friend in Kohima, peace advocate Charles Chasie, also made constructive comments.

Colin Whurr, my publishing colleague and friend of thirty-five years, enthusiastically submitted the manuscript in its first draft to three publishers. I am grateful to him and also indebted to the publishers who unconsciously did me a service by turning it down. Knowing something about the economics of publishing, I understood their decisions, which led me to recast and extend the manuscript, and explore the idea that it should be published by the Kohima Educational Trust on the understanding that the gross profits would go to the Trust's cause. Major General Murray Naylor, Chairman of the Trust, and Robert Lyman, Treasurer, warmly accepted this idea and recommended acceptance to their fellow trustees.

For protection against the toils and pitfalls of self-publishing, I am deeply indebted to Douglas Williamson, editor, designer and production expert. He and I agreed that we would make a beautiful book. He has done so and has been a joy to work with.

When I was a newspaper correspondent more than half a century ago, I used to type my stories. I found that deadlines and the chatter of the keys made a stimulating combination. In my latter years, I have become lazy, and I have time. So I dictate drafts and then work them over several times in my not very legible handwriting. Turning these into clean copy has been painstakingly accomplished by my skilful and patient secretary, Margaret Mills.

Finally, to my wife Betty, who has patiently suffered my abstraction for hours and days; creates the atmosphere in which I am able to indulge my attempts at creativity; provides the life support that keeps me going; and emancipates me from innumerable tasks, I owe more than words can tell.

Select Bibliography

MEMOIRS

GRANT, Peter *A Highlander Goes to War* Pentland Press, 1955

KING-CLARK, R *The Battle for Kohima: the narrative of the 2nd Battalion the Manchester Regiment* Fleur de Lys Publishing, 1995

WILSON, Leslie *A Son of the Raj* Pentland Press, 1996

HISTORIES

CAMPBELL, Arthur *The Siege* Allen & Unwin, 1956

COLVIN, John *No Ordinary Men* Leo Cooper, 1995

HART, Peter *At the Sharp End: from Le Paradis to Kohima* Leo Cooper: Pen & Sword Books, 1998

HAVERS, Norman *March On! An infantry battalion in England, India and Burma* Square One, 1992

PHILLIPS, C E Lucas *Springboard to Victory: Battle for Kohima* Heinemann 1966

ROONEY, David *Burma Victory: Imphal, Kohima and the Chindit issue* Arms and Armour Press, 1992

SEAMAN, Harry *The Battle at Sangshak* Leo Cooper, 1989

SWINSON, Arthur *Kohima* Arrow Books, 1968 / Cassell, 1996

WHITE, O G W *Straight on for Tokyo* Gale & Polden 1948

THE NAGAS

BOWER, Ursula Graham *Naga Path* Murray, 1950

CHASIE, Charles *The Naga Imbroglio* Standard Printers & Publishers, Kohima, May 1999

The above list is confined to books concerned substantially with the Battle of Kohima and the campaign of the 2nd Division. For a comprehensive collection of over a thousand titles on the Burma Campaign, readers are referred to the descriptive catalogue and bibliography of the Burma Campaign Memorial Library, obtainable from the Library of the School of Oriental and African Studies, Thornhaugh Street, Russell Square, London WC1H 0XG.

INDEX

Note: page numbers in *italics* refer to illustrations

145